T0283542

I was laughing so hard I honestly could not catch my breath! I've seen him many times since, and I get just as tickled as I did that first time. I know the punch lines now, but the combination of his hilarious, clean material, his facial expressions, and his impeccable sense of timing still makes me laugh. Uncontrollably. I can't wait to read his book."

–Bill Anderson, Grand Ole Opry Country Music Hall of Fame, Nashville, Tennessee

"For over forty years, James Gregory's humor has been a cornerstone of the StarDome, enchanting generations. Witnessing his journey has been a privilege and a joy, a testament to the timeless bond of laughter."

–Bruce Ayers, owner of The StarDome in Birmingham, Alabama

"'The Funniest Man in America' is not just James Gregory's slogan, it's the truth! I don't care how many times I've heard James' jokes, they're always just as funny as the first time. He is a master showman, legendary comedian whose comedy is real and timeless.

–Keith Bilbrey (voice of the *Grand Ole Opry*, announcer for *The Huckabee Show*)

"This is a tough business. An ultimate professional like James makes all the difference in the world to a comedy club like mine. James has been a true asset to me, and I value our friendship and relationship immensely. James has always been at the top of my list of favorite comedians to deal with."

–Jordan Hawley, owner of Comedy off Broadway in Lexington, Kentucky

And From The Fans...

"I never had a real family, but you, Mr. Gregory, made me a part of yours with your delightful way of bringing back memories of your own family. I love you dearly."

–"Alec" from Mississippi

"I call it commonsense comedy. Always makes me laugh and it's too bad you're not running for president!"

–James Johnson, Dubois, Wyoming

"Always makes me laugh on some of my worst days. It never grows old. Pure, clean enjoyment. You are truly the Funniest Man in America. The best!"

–David Watkins, Marble, North Carolina

A BUSHEL OF BEANS AND A PECK OF TOMATOES

A BUSHEL OF BEANS AND A PECK OF TOMATOES

The Life and Times of "The Funniest Man in America"

JAMES GREGORY

with Michael E. Long

PERMUTED
PRESS

A PERMUTED PRESS BOOK
ISBN: 979-8-88845-425-1
ISBN (eBook): 979-8-88845-426-8

PERMUTED
PRESS

Permuted Press
New York • Nashville
permutedpress.com

Published in the United States of America
1 2 3 4 5 6 7 8 9 10

A NOTE TO THE READER

On May 9, 2024, James Gregory passed away.

It was a peaceful trip home, with family around. I'm sure you're pleased to know that, and James would want you to know. He'd been battling a heart condition and related issues for several years. He'd beaten them before but this time it was just too much.

James earned his rest, but what he really wanted in his final days was to be back in front of all y'all—his "customers," as he'd say. He thought of you not as fans but as friends and family, but you probably already knew that. As much as he matters to you folks, you mattered to him just as much. He loved you all. He loved putting on his show for you. He loved how you wanted to hear the old routines as much as you wanted to hear the new stuff. He loved talking with you after the show until the club owner made everybody go home. He loved running into you at Waffle House or Cracker Barrel, signing something, taking a photo, even standing next to you when you'd call up your uncle and say, "You'll never guess who I'm with right now!"

But most of all he loved working behind that microphone and hearing all of you laugh and laugh.

This book was very important to him. As his co-author, I can tell you there were times he wrestled over every word. I'm the fortunate man who got to sit with him for hours, in person and by phone, going through the details of his life from Lithonia, Georgia, on. It was an honor. My friend James wanted this book to be special, and it is. In fact, it was the last "professional" assignment he did before he left. Three days before he passed, he was sitting with his manager and close, longtime friend, Lenny Sisselman, personally writing captions for the photographs—and he'd picked out those pictures himself only a few days earlier.

This book exists because James wanted you to know the real story. Sure, there are laughs in here, but he wanted all of you to know the rest: where he came from, how he grew up, what he did before he was a comedian, what his life was like on the road and as a businessman—he wanted to give you the whole picture, the man behind all those hilarious routines.

I would never presume to speak for James, but I will on just one thing: He cared more about all of you than you can ever imagine. He was grateful for every one of you, and he loved you.

And that's the real story of James Gregory.

Michael E. Long
July 2024

IN MEMORIAM

The saying "Laughter is the best medicine" is believed to have originated from Proverbs 17:22 of the King James Bible. But it's more than a proverb. The power of laughter has long been recognized by both medical and spiritual experts.

King Solomon wrote in Ecclesiastes 3:4 that in life, there is "a time to weep and a time to laugh…" So when it's time to laugh, laugh! And know God is laughing with you.

I have said in recent years, not in a public forum but in private conversations, that the real funniest man in America left this world February 26, 2014! I know I will see him again eventually. But I'm in no hurry to get there. I know once I get there, I'll just be one of the "opening" acts. Because no one, absolutely no one, can follow Tim Wilson!

CONTENTS

FOREWORD BY DEAN GAINES

How do I begin to share my journey with James? What words can express a chance meeting that would change my life forever? James and I had so much in common, even though we would not meet until the early '80s. You must understand the times. The internet didn't exist, nor did cell phones for many years. These were things left to the imagination of science fiction movies. Many, if not all, of the most famous names in comedy today had not yet done their first show. Even now, when I spend time with James, we revisit the sequence of the following events; we must acknowledge divine intervention.

James Gregory Jr., the child of proud Southerners, was born in the muddy red hills of Georgia. I can still hear the kind tone of his mother's voice saying, "Hold on for a minute. You must be calling for James. Here's his number and the hotel where he's staying."

The chance meeting in the early 1980s was during the comedy boom. Clubs were popping up in every town across America. You see, comedy clubs had amateur nights. Zanies Nashville was on Tuesday night, like the Punchline in Atlanta and the Knoxville Funny Bone. The original Comedy Catch Chattanooga was on Wednesday night. I took the elevator to the top floor and walked in on a Wednesday night; a group of local amateurs were to my right. There was a long, twenty-foot bar to my left, and eight barstools down was the headliner for the week, a comedian from Atlanta, Georgia. He was wearing a diamond earring and had a cigarette in one hand, and bitters and soda in the other.

How did one night have such a lasting impact so many years later? Because, with just a few kind words, he saved my life. I came off the stage, and this headlining Atlanta comedian said, "You're funny. Are you working anywhere?" I said no. He looked at me and said, "We're going to fix that. Yes, sir, we're going to fix that." At this time, I was trying to find a way out, a sense of urgency born after a year of unpaid amateur nights.

The next day, I met James for lunch, with twenty-eighty dollars to my name. I remember hoping I could cover the lunch. After lunch, James picked up the phone and called one of the biggest agents in the Southeast. After that call, I was booked for 111 one-nighters in a row. He picked up the phone again and called the Punchline owners. On his word, they booked me into all of their clubs, and the relationships that he had built with other club owners through phone calls on my behalf across America.

As I write this, I am looking back over eleven thousand shows, having had the opportunity to work with some of the greatest comedians. The best way to describe forty years is that I've met everyone but Elvis, but his closest friends became mine. I have traveled all over the world. You see, that chance meeting allowed me to meet Mr. Sinatra at Resorts Atlantic City, Sammy in Vegas, Norm Crosby, Steve Allen, Frank Gorshin, and Phyllis Diller. Comedy has generational moves. You can see our graduating class if you will. Here is the roll call of the comedians I know because I was there! This list can't be challenged or denied: J. Anthony Brown, Jeff Foxworthy, Steve Harvey, David Saye, Kip Addotta, Ron White, Carrot Top, Ray Romano, Diane Ford, Jerry Seinfeld, John Fox, Bill Hicks, Ollie Joe Prater, Bernie Mac, DC Curry,

George Wallace, Tim Wilson, Jimmy Walker, Jeff Cesario, Henry Cho, Bill Engvall, Frankie Bastille, Tim Allen, Dennis Miller, Thea Vidale, Emo Phillips, and Ken Rogerson.

This unique fraternity of real comedians must have a valedictorian! James is the first in this class of modern comedians to self-promote and market himself by mail in America. He was the first in our industry to merchandise his likeness and image in the early 1980s. A visionary long before the internet. James is a proud marine, lover of God and country, and, most importantly, the son of the Gregorys of Lithonia, Georgia.

The kindness James showed me all those years ago allows me to reciprocate to others. The good that I've been able to accomplish is because of James. There's an old saying back home in Tennessee that if you ever see a turtle on top of a twenty-foot pole, he didn't get there by himself.

James Gregory saved my life. He helped me stand when I could not stand on my own. He reached down and lifted me. Thank you, my dearest friend. You've said it at the end of every phone call over the last forty years. And now I say it to you: I love you, James.

KID STUFF

I've had an amazing life. What makes it even more amazing to me is this: I didn't choose the comedy business. I fell into it.

Most comedians get started when they're in their twenties. Some get up on stage for the first time when they're teenagers, a few while they're still in high school.

Not me. I was thirty-six.

That's kinda crazy. There are thirty-six-year-old comedians out there now who've been at it nearly twenty years. When I got up on stage for the first time, I'd been working longer than that at a bunch of jobs, and none of them were in comedy. In fact, I got my first real job when I was eleven. That was twenty-five years before!

But I'm already getting ahead of myself.

I'd always been a fan of comedians and comedy, but never in my life did I think, "I'd love to be in showbiz." Never occurred to me when I was a kid, never in high school, never when I was a young man. When you're a little kid living in a wide spot in the road in Georgia in the 1950s, and you're thinking about what you're going to be when you grow up, comedian isn't the first thing that crosses your mind.

If your daddy's a fireman or your mama fixes hair, you'll probably say something like that. Whatever the job, if you don't know a grownup already doing it, you won't think of it for yourself. Whatever you're gonna be is something you've already seen.

When I ended up in comedy, years later, it was partially because the seed got planted early on. When I was in grade school and high school, the most popular shows on television were variety shows like *The Red Skelton Show* and *The Jack Benny Show*. These were the kinds of thing you don't see on TV anymore. They'd have solo singers, musical groups, dancers, once in a while there'd be a magician, and every week there'd be novelty acts like a juggler or a guy who spins plates on top of long poles. (If you think that sounds stupid now, it looked even stupider back then. I don't know what they were thinking.)

One variety show was bigger than all of them, *The Ed Sullivan Show*. It went on the air in 1948 and ran for twenty-four years. They performed it live from New York City, and from the same theater David Letterman would eventually use for his *Late Show*. Every week, Ed would have on a comedian, guys like Alan King, Jackie Mason, Jack E. Leonard, Jack Carter, and Jan Murray. My dad loved comedians and he never missed whoever Ed had on each week. Dad and I would sit there together and watch—and laugh and laugh.

Of course, once the comedian was done, my dad would change the channel. He didn't care about the rest.

It would be years before that love of comedy turned into any idea at all about being in the comedy business myself. It'd be quite a while before I got around to that.

I got my first job in the spring of 1957, when I was eleven. It was in an old country grocery store, and they let me work a couple hours after school. To appreciate that, you have to understand that we lived out in the country.

Back then, most people in the US lived in rural areas. That's not like now. For the great majority of people in the twenty-first century, they live in or around a big city. Pretty much everybody they know lives that way, too. But back then, it was the other way around. Life was different.

In those days, people acted differently. We looked at the world and the culture and politics differently, too. Even what we saw every day was different from what we all see today. Try to visualize no interstate—I mean literally no interstate, 'cause they hadn't been built yet. I grew up on a dirt road called Turner Hill Road. For a lot of people, that was the rule, not the exception. We were part of a community of people who lived nearby, and it really was a community of friends and neighbors and family.

The world was smaller. That wasn't a bad thing. It was just the way it was. That country market where I got my first job was not a supermarket. It was a grocery with a few aisles and a little counter with one mechanical register where you'd check out.

I would get off school and be home at 3:15, and I could walk that couple of miles to the store pretty easily. I'd get to work by four o'clock, which was when I had to be there. I worked four to nine on Monday and Friday, and on Saturday I worked from nine in the morning until one in the afternoon. The store was closed on Wednesday, but they had me come in anyway. I'd unload the stuff they brought from the warehouse and restock the store. As I got older, maybe sixteen or seventeen, they gave me a few more hours. I was a reliable worker, especially for a kid.

The pay wasn't bad, either. When I first started, they paid me five dollars a week. After a couple of years, I made it up to ten dollars a week. I know that doesn't seem like much. I'll talk to other comedians about my first job and when I get to the part about the pay, they always ask me how in the world I could work a week for five dollars.

Here's how: five dollars in 1958 is like fifty dollars today.

For a nickel or a dime, you could get anything that you wanted. Candy bars were a nickel. You could pull a bottle of soda out of the machine for a dime. (You didn't press a button. The soda machine was loaded with glass bottles on their sides. You put in your coin and that opened a little gate that held back the bottle. You'd pull it over that bump, and you had to pull it hard, and you'd have your cold drink.) So for a kid in 1958, five dollars a week was a lot of money.

But that job meant more to me than candy bars and Coca-Colas. I wanted that job and I needed that job because I grew up extremely, extremely poor.

I didn't want to be completely broke.

More important, I didn't want to feel like that. My first job was the first step to changing it. I'll never forget those two feelings, the one before I had a job, and the one after I started. I had that job until I got my high school diploma. That was a big day for everybody in the family, not just me, because I was the first Gregory to graduate from high school.

At that point, I started looking for my first full-time job. I wanted more money in my pocket, more security for my future, and to get on the path to a better life.

JAMES GREGORY, WORKING MAN

When I was eighteen, I took a civil service exam so I could work at the post office. I passed and got the job, but they didn't make me a carrier. I sorted mail at the old post office on Forsythe Street in downtown Atlanta. I was working the third shift, 11:30 in the evening until eight in the morning, with thirty minutes for lunch—but since lunch was at 3 a.m., I don't know if lunch is the best word for it.

I was a civil servant. This was a big deal at my house. All I was doing was sorting mail, but to hear my kinfolks tell it, I was like a lawyer or a doctor. Being the first Gregory with that high school diploma had already paid off because I couldn't have gotten the job without it.

The pride I had in that job is another example of how the world has changed. College wasn't the obvious next step after high school. Only one or two out of ten kids would go to college, depending on the part of the country you were in. Unlike today, they didn't go away to school to spend tens of thousands of dollars to "grow up." They went so they could learn how to do something you could learn only at a university: to be a lawyer, a doctor, maybe an accountant, something like that.

Like I said, not everybody graduated in the first place. It was pretty common at the age of fourteen, fifteen, or sixteen to quit school and go to work right away, to help support the family or to start your own—in those days, people got married younger, even in their teens. A high school senior with a wife or a husband was not unheard of. This was 1964. Things were different.

I worked at the post office until 1968, then they transferred me to the Department of Defense, but I was still sorting mail. This was the first step in my illustrious and brief military career.

In 1968, the Vietnam War was at its peak. At the Department of Defense, my job was to make sure the mail got to the right people. Every day, I'd attack a big bag of mail.

The draft was in full swing. I had so far avoided receiving an invitation in my own mail. There were ways to avoid being drafted, of course. One of them was to sign up yourself. At least that way you might have more say over where they put you. One of my coworkers, Fred Anderson, started talking about doing exactly that. He wanted to be in the army, maybe even the marines. For some crazy reason, I decided that's what I oughta do, too. So in 1968, I joined up. They sent me where they sent every new marine: twelve weeks on Parris Island, South Carolina, for what I guess you'd call boot camp.

A week before I was supposed to graduate from basic training, I was standing in the chow line when I collapsed. I was passed out cold; whether it was for five seconds or five minutes, I don't know. When I woke up, they had me on a stretcher and were taking me to sickbay.

For some reason, I was twitching, so at first, they thought maybe I was having an epileptic seizure. They couldn't figure it out, so they put me in the military hospital in Charleston and kept me there for a couple weeks. My family came up to visit me. Long story short, they never figured it out, so they discharged me. But I did get close enough to graduating that I did get all my pictures made in my dress blues. I still have that picture!

To this day, I don't know exactly what the problem was. I had high blood pressure, that's for sure, and I was on medication when I was discharged. But whatever the problem was, the problem went away, and it was probably that combined with heat exhaustion. This happened in August, and it was hot on Parris Island. Given what was going on in Vietnam at that time, I guess I was lucky that I did collapse. If I hadn't passed out that day, I would have ended up in Vietnam.

IT WAS ALMOST MY CAREER

I was out of the Marine Corps, but I didn't want to go back to civil service. There were a lot of benefits to it as far as retirement and all that kind of stuff, but I got to thinking about where I spent every day. The office I stayed in was very small, just a small room. There were four coworkers and we'd meet a few other people, and everything was like a routine to me. Eat at a certain hour, you'd have thirty minutes for lunch. Just a routine routine. There was a gray metal desk and a black telephone. And I got to thinking about this. *Is this something that I want to do for twenty-five years just so I'll have a good pension? Is that what this is all about?*

So I started looking for jobs and I found one in the bookkeeping department at the Atlanta Blueprint Company. I did really well, and one of the guys that owned the place paid for me to go to night school to learn more about bookkeeping. I stayed there through 1968, 69, and 70.

As for the money, it was great. When I talk about this, you have to keep the time in mind. When I started working at the Atlanta Blueprint Company, they paid me $150 a week. That came out to be about $3.75 an hour, and that was more than double the minimum wage at the time. When the post office hired me years before in 1964, in civil service, my pay was $2.26 an hour, and that was double the minimum wage at that time, too. So I had gotten used to having a good job.

Then I saw an ad for part-time sales work, commission only. This was the kind of sales where you go into people's homes and sell overpriced things like encyclopedias. You'd always deal with some mister and missus and come to their house after five in the evening. I took that job and I started making more money at part-time sales than I did at Atlanta Blueprint Company, so I quit my job as a full-time employee and I started working sales with commission only, no draw. I made only what I earned. You might say it was like "If you don't work, you don't eat."

That was a turning point in my life. Starting with that job in 1971 and ever since, I've been a 1099 person. I would never again be anybody's full-time employee. Instead of receiving a W-2 form where they took out my taxes for me and paid me a fixed amount every week, I'd be an independent contractor with a yearly 1099-MISC form. I don't get paid because somebody gives me a salary. I get paid because I sold them the benefit of what I can do.

(I also take out my own taxes and pay them quarterly. If everybody had to do that instead of the boss taking them out and sending in the check so you don't notice, the country would have a revolt. The government would lower taxes before sunset.)

Not long after, they offered me the opportunity to go to Indiana and be the branch manager in the town of Anderson, not very far from Indianapolis. I was over the salesmen at that office who were working towns like Kokomo, Terre Haute, and others, and I was still working on percentage—commission only, no base salary at all, the way I liked it then and like it now. I was there from 1971 to 1978, then back to headquarters down to Atlanta, back where I began.

In 1980, the two people who owned that business changed their focus. Now they were selling Lincoln Log home franchises, based in Charlotte, and they offered me an opportunity to go to Charlotte to be a part of that. I decided to take a few months off, not so much as a vacation but for an opportunity to make money and combine it with a vacation. A guy I worked with in Indiana was going to work with a different sales group in Tampa, Florida, so I went to Tampa for a few months to make a few dollars and treat that like a vacation. I stayed there until 1981.

I was a good salesman. I made good money at it. I had job security. And I liked doing it. I could have gone far with it—I'd already done pretty well—and it very well could have been my career for the rest of my life.

But then, something happened that I did not expect and was not looking for. And I stumbled into the job—the career, really-ly—I'd pursue for the rest of my life.

Here's the Story: Fill It Up

People ask me all the time, where do you get the ideas for your routines? I get 'em everywhere! So I decided to go through my material and tell you where some of my most popular stuff came from. I call these sections "Here's the Story." I hope you like 'em. To see me tell the original story, use your phone to capture the QR code below, and it'll take you right to it! – James

***

"I don't wanna die in a plane crash because some fat woman lied about her weight!"

I say the story took place in the Bahamas, but actually it happened in Texas. It was the late 1980s, and a guy who had seen me perform asked me to come in for a corporate event there. It was a regional meeting for Walmart and was one of my first corporate gigs ever. I was on the bill with Joe Diffie, a popular country music artist at the time who has since passed away.

I flew to Dallas-Fort Worth. From there I had switch planes to fly to Amarillo, which is a small airport. They had arranged a private flight for me. It was on a little plane, one with propellors. There was one other guy besides me and he was the pilot—no copilot at all. This was a short flight, only about ninety minutes, and the weather was rough. I don't like to fly anyway, so I made a joke to this guy. "What would happen if you had a heart attack?"

He said, "Then we both die!" and he laughed.

I said, "That ain't funny!"

Then he said, "This plane doesn't hold but one passenger. How much do you weigh?"

I said, "I don't know."

"I hope you're not too fat. I'm kinda fat. Two fat people could die. I hope I have enough fuel!"

I said, "Fill it up!"

EXCELSIOR MILL

The story about me getting into the comedy business is kind of bizarre.

When I came out of Tampa, I was trying to make up my mind whether to go to Charlotte or back to Indianapolis. In the meantime, I was hanging out at my parents' house for a while and I was bored.

I've always been a news reader. I need to see a newspaper every day. It was 1981 and I was in Scottdale, a suburb of Atlanta, and I'd walk around and find a paper. Used to be that they sold them out of a rack where you'd put a quarter in. On this day, the rack was empty, but right next to it was another rack that had a huge newspaper in it called *Creative Loafing*, and it was free. I'd never read it but I picked it up just to have something to do. I took it back to the house and came across an ad for a place called Excelsior Mill that was going to start doing comedy.

Excelsior Mill was called that because it used to be where a cotton mill was located. The two guys who ran the place were Mike Reeves and Matt McCoy. They'd made it into a restaurant, a really good one, and the ad said that they were about to start a comedy workshop in the basement on Sunday nights. The ad said that if you ever thought you'd like to be a comedian, here's a phone number you can call.

In the sales business, we'd have big sales conferences because it was a nationwide operation. We would meet in Kansas City and places like that. As one of the speakers, I could make the audience laugh. I always thought I was funny, so when I read this thing about comedy at Excelsior Mill, I said, "Yeah, I think I'll go." When I called, the guy who answered said, "You don't have to be funny!" I think at this point, he was desperate to have anybody up there on stage for entertainment. There were no expectations on anybody's part, and nobody was getting paid, of course. We went to the Excelsior Mill show just to get on stage, to be funny, and to have a good time hanging out with each other. This show became a regular Sunday night thing. I enjoyed it, I met a lot of people there, and some of them are still my friends to this day.

I did that for almost a year before something happened that would change things for me.

***

In 1982, the Punchline in Atlanta, Georgia opened up. That was a big event, and not just for me. Prior to 1982 the only place where you could go see live stand-up comedians was Los Angeles, San Francisco, Chicago, Boston, New York City, or some other very big city. If you lived anywhere else, there was no such thing as saying to your wife or your girlfriend, "Let's go see a comedian tonight." You couldn't. The clubs did not exist. This new club changed all that. It was the very first place in the Southeast where you could see comedians anywhere besides TV. This was professional comedy in a club setting.

The guys who opened it, Ron DiNunzio and Dave Montesano, put their club in what used to be, at various times, a carpet store, and a country and western bar. The new place would turn out to be a launching pad for a lot of comedians, many who would become household names. It would turn out to be a big deal for me, too. Here's how I found out about it.

Every comedy club has the same format: an opening act, a feature act, and a headliner. When Ron and Dave opened up the Punchline, they knew they were gonna have to fly in a headliner, but they would find the opener and the feature locally. That's where I come in.

In 1982, the internet did not exist. Publicity was all newspaper, newspaper, newspaper. Every Saturday, the *Atlanta Journal Constitution* had an entertainment section that covered whatever was going on around the city: movies, plays, sports games, what have you. The *Atlanta Journal* sent a reporter to Excelsior Mill to do a story about these people working every Sunday night who wanted to be comedians. The day he came out, I happened to have on a red shirt, and that was enough to get me on the cover. Turns out that was all the attention I needed for what happened next.

Ron and Dave came across the story and two names popped out, mine and J. Anthony Brown's. They got hold of me at my parents' phone number and called J. Anthony, too, and the next day, he and I headed down to meet them. Ron brought us upstairs to his office and told us why we were there. For their big opening, they'd hired a headliner, Marc Weiner and the Weinerettes, which was a very successful ventriloquist act at the time. (Marc is still working today and he does a lot of TV, especially for kids.) They needed a feature performer to go on in front of him, and an opening act to go up first and emcee the show.

J. Anthony and I didn't fully appreciate that the feature slot was higher up the ladder than the emcee, and that later, if we ended up going on the road, the feature makes more money. We didn't know any of that, so we had no way to decide who should take one position and who should take the other. Ron said we ought to just flip a coin.

I said heads. It came up tails. And that's how J. Anthony Brown got to start his career, as a feature, not having to work as an opener, and how I started out as the opener, having to work my way up to feature. Pure, dumb luck. That coin flip cost me money. I had to start in the business as an opening act, which is what everybody does—but J. Anthony is the only comedian I know who started as a feature, maybe the only comedian anybody knows who did that.

I had a gut feeling that I could be successful in the comedy business. I was only an opening act, but I felt that I was on the right path. To anybody else, though it could not have looked that way at all. Either way, on Wednesday, February 17, 1982, I became the first stand-up comedian to take the stage at the brand-new Atlanta Punchline, one of the first comedy clubs outside New York or LA.

BROKE IN THE BACK SEAT

You may be surprised to find out that when it comes to funny business, I'm a serious man.

Comedy is my job, so I work very hard at it and I try to be the best—or at least the Funniest Man in America. You pay to see me. You deserve to get your money's worth. The way I see it, you're not just my audience. You're my customers. I want you satisfied—more than satisfied! But I'd feel that way no matter what my job was.

This is my philosophy of life: Provide for yourself. Help people who need help—absolutely. Be generous. But your first responsibility is to make sure nobody has to take care of you. That makes the world work a lot more easily. Look after your own needs.

It took a long time for me to completely live that way, but I can honestly say that I was on the path to responsibility and independence from early on. I have always been committed to working, to doing something with my time and my life. That's why I've been employed every consecutive year for the past six decades.

At thirty-five, I moved back in with my parents. I wasn't making much money at comedy. As an opening act, I was making only $300 or $350 a week, and the only place I could work and get paid as an opener was Atlanta. This was 1982 when the Punchline opened there. In 1982, I made $3,200 for the year. In 1983, as other clubs started to open in Alabama, North and South Carolina, and Tennessee, I made $12,000, still at $300 or $350 a week, and for nine shows a week: one show on Tuesday, one on Wednesday, one on Thursday, two on Friday, three on Saturday, and one to close out the week on Sunday. We liked when we'd work in South Carolina because in those days the state still had what were called "blue laws," meaning they couldn't sell alcohol on Sunday. That meant we could do the last show on Saturday night and go home a day early.

In 1983, the Punchline in Columbia, South Carolina had been open only a few weeks, and they hadn't found a condo yet so they put the comedians in a motel. I was the opening act, Dennis Miller was the feature, and Dave Coulier (who would soon star on *Full House*) was the headliner. The club owner, Robert "Robo" Walker, phoned me at the motel—there were no cell phones in those days—to ask me to bring along the other two comedians from the motel to the club. For this trip, I had borrowed my dad's pickup. Dennis and Dave came up to me and thanked me for the ride, but then Dennis looked up and down at Dad's old truck. He said, "We gotta ride in that?"

"Nah," I said, and I laughed. "You can call a cab if you want."

Well, Dennis went along anyway, and the three of us crowded in. Dave used props in his act and in those days, believe it or not, Dennis had a few, too, so we piled all that in the bed of the truck and made the trip together every night that week.

By the end of the week, Dennis had changed his tune. As we split up after the last show, he shook my hand and took one more look up and down that old truck, then he said. "I tell ya, James, I may have to buy a pickup truck myself!"

Then there was what happened in Oklahoma the next year, 1984. When I think back on those days, I get emotional. This was one of the most important moments of my life.

***

I used to go to Oklahoma as an opening act. I'd make $400 for the week. That was fifty dollars more than other places, but not the whole fifty bucks more. I had to pay a 10 percent fee to a booking agent named Chris DiPetta, a great guy then and now, but I sure could've used the extra few dollars in those days. I'd get a little break because they'd book me two weeks in a row down there, one week in Tulsa, one in Oklahoma City, so I could stay down there twice as long as a usual gig before I had to come back. Bottom line, Oklahoma meant I traveled farther and longer for an extra ten bucks a week.

I wasn't clearing any money for the work so I couldn't afford to fly. Since I couldn't afford a motel, either, I kept a blanket and a pillow in the back seat of my car because I would have to spend the night in the rest area. In the summertime it was an oven. In the wintertime I froze to death. That's the part where the memories come back in a big way.

Every time I was in the back seat of that car, freezing to death (and not in a comical way—I was genuinely freezing), the only thing I kept saying to myself was *What the hell are you doing?*

I had made great money in the sales business. I always had cash in my pocket, always drove a new car, had a nice apartment. With one phone call, I could go right back to a good job and a steady income—a whole lot more than I was making as a comedian, and a whole lot less struggle. And now, here I was, mooching off my parents and barely getting by. I had nothing going that would indicate this was a wise decision. But there was something—it was just…it's just in your gut.

Maybe that comes from the fact that I'd already had "real" jobs. I understood the difference between playing at something and really working at it. A lot of comedians did not. Working the road, I'd meet guys had who been in the business six years, eight years, twelve years. They were still broke. They had the same work habits, year after year. At the end of the show, they'd hang out at the bar until the club closed. At the end of the week, they'd get paid, and their bar tab would be almost as much as their salary. They treated all this like it was a party—not all of them, but most of them. *What's the point for them?*

Then I had this thought: *What's the point for me?*

That's when I started to realize: This is not party time.

This is not just something to have fun with.

This. Is. My. Job.

That freezing night, shivering and broke in the back of my car and wondering why I wasn't back in a sales job somewhere, with my own roof over my head, and money in my pocket—that night, by the side of the road, I figured it out: this was my job and I was not there for playtime. I was there to build a career, and that requires sacrifice.

That's why, when I talk about the comedy business, I do not use the word "passion." All the other comedians I met out there use that word, but not me.

In the 1980s, so many of these comedians would say their passion was comedy, but I don't think it was. Their passion was avoiding day work. I'd hear them talking about this even on stage. A feature act might say, *I love this job! I only work thirty minutes a day.* And they'd start to believe that. But they were wrong.

When you do what we were doing, you were actually working more hours than a regular, full-time job, a lot more than forty hours a week. Think about it. Wherever you go, you have to get there. Then you have to get back. And where are you? You're in a condo. Not at your home. Not with your girlfriend. Not with your wife. Not with your children. You are not at home. You are on the road—you are at work.

So we were putting in a lot more than forty hours. In my mind, it was twenty-four hours a day. But most of these guys had convinced themselves they were working less than an hour a day. I was determined to do it differently and to have a different attitude about it because it's the only way that works. Most comedians don't really want to hear this. I think it's because the advice I give them is based on reality. I remember talking about this at my house to a friend of mine who is a very successful comedian. You'd know the name. He's done Letterman twice, Kimmel once. I was talking about the business side of comedy when he said, "I've never been one of those people obsessed with money."

I said, "Are you implying that I'm obsessed with money?" He gave me this look like he didn't understand. I said, "I have never been obsessed with money, but I'll tell you who is. Every car dealer I've ever dealt with. Every jeweler I've ever dealt with.

"Go to the supermarket and load up your cart, then go to the cashier. Show her a tape of you on *The David Letterman Show*. She'll laugh. She'll probably call over the other cashiers and say, *Look! This guy's a comedian.* They'll all laugh, too. But they will not let you walk out those doors until you give them some money.

"Your girlfriend, your boyfriend, your wife, your husband. It's their anniversary, their birthday. You go to the jewelry store to buy them something nice. The clerk gets out a wristwatch and puts it on the counter. Now, tell them how funny you are. Tell them you've been on television. You'll get all kinds of compliments, but if that's all you give them you will not leave that jewelry store with that watch.

"Those people? They're obsessed with money, so you better start making some. They'll give you all the applause you want, but if they're not getting paid then you're not walking out of there with anything. So when you say money doesn't matter to you, that's not how the world works. You say you're not obsessed with money? Why would that be something to brag about?"

I don't think my friend wanted to hear that. I don't think many people in show business wanna hear it, either. The bottom line is getting paid for what you do. That's not being obsessed with money in a bad way. That's recognizing how the world works.

THE INTERSECTION OF
WISH AND HOPE

It's good to be optimistic, but it's not good to be delusional.

Spencer Tracy was a great actor, very famous, and a natural in front of the camera. He passed away more than fifty years ago, but what he said about show business is just as valuable today as it was when he said it. He understood just how important—or, I should say, not important—show business really is.

Spencer Tracy said that all of us in this business are lucky. The American people need plumbers, they need electricians, they need truck drivers, they need landscapers, but they don't need us. The very idea that we can make a living playacting? We're all just lucky, he said, so we better not let all this attention go to our heads too much. A good plumber is a lot more valuable than a good actor. That's Spencer Tracy talking. This is me: Maybe you work at a job like this, and maybe you don't work too hard at it. That'll make you forget something important: your money may be coming easy for now, but that's not how the world works for everybody else. In fact, the world can do without what we do for a living.

Enjoy what you do, enjoy what you have, and be optimistic about what's ahead, but don't be delusional about your place in the world. Being famous as an entertainer can make us a lot of things, but mostly what it means is we got lucky.

That's not gonna stop anybody from dreaming about being a comedian or from trying to make a career in show business. And it shouldn't discourage anybody. If that's what you want, go for it. But "go for it" has to mean "work for it." It doesn't mean sit around and talk about how great it's gonna be when it happens. I talk about wish and hope. We should have hope. Without hope, why would we wake up tomorrow? But we can't rely on hope. Of course I hope I win the lottery. That's why I bought the ticket. But I can't conduct my life and assume I'm going to win the lottery. That would be foolish.

If you stay on the reality highway, you'll probably get to where you want to go. But what happens to most people is they're traveling down the reality highway, they get to where it crosses the intersection of wish and hope, and they take one of those turns. And that's the wrong turn. You can go for a little while down Hope Avenue on one side or Wish Road on the other. Enjoy it! Pull over and find a picnic table. Sit in the shade. Have a cigar! Enjoy the view. But stay there too long and you'll never reach your destination. You better get back in the car and head back to the reality highway right away. 'Cause if you stay on Wish Avenue too long, you will get lost. You need to be on that reality highway, 'cause that's going someplace in reality. Wish and hope look like they go to some wonderful places. Problem is, those places aren't real. To get there you have to stick to reality all the way. We all have to.

Most people who are in the world of show business, and those who want to be, talk about pursuing their dream. Myself, I don't use the word dream. I use the word goal. I prefer that, as in *What's your goal?* A dream is something nice to think about, but just the fact that you call it a dream makes it more like something imaginary. That's no way to get through life, dreaming about a dream. I prefer the word goal. You can't make a plan to reach a dream, but you sure as hell can plan to reach a goal. A goal is real, and a plan will get you there.

But a goal without a plan isn't even a dream. It's just a wish.

In all the years of my life, one of the first things I learned has also been the most useful: get yourself a goal and work for it. *Here's my goal. What am I gonna do about it?*

There's nothing wrong with dreams. But with dreams, at some point, you wake up. I was an opening act, I had no money, and I didn't have enough work as a comedian to have my own place or pay my own way. But being in that position changed my life and my philosophy completely from what it used to be.

Before I ended up almost broke and living at my parents' house, I had been making really good money in the sales business. I wasn't relying on a guaranteed salary, either. It was pure commission: if I didn't work, I didn't eat. Turned out I was pretty good at that. This was the early 1970s, and the average household income in the US—not per person but for an entire household—was about $12,000 a year. Compare that to what I was making in sales: about $22,000 a year. All that was for one person, me, a single guy in his twenties. That may not sound like much, but remember that we're talking fifty years ago. In today's dollars, I was making as much as $160,000 a year, over $13,000 a month.

I was living like it, too. Truth is, as soon as I started working in civil service, I had more money than I'd ever had in my life. Growing up so poor, with no new clothes, no extras, not much of anything more than the basics, you might say I went crazy with it. Then, when I became a salesman, working on commission meant I could make as much as I was willing to work for, and I bought myself even more. The first thing I wanted was a brand-new car.

I bought a 1965 Chevy Super Sport—$500 down, seventy-two dollars a month for three years. That car was yellow with a black interior, and fully loaded. A couple years later, I traded it for a 1966 Plymouth Fury, maroon. It was such a great car that a coworker of mine bought one for himself. Of course, pretty soon I was ready for something else, so I sold it with less than twenty thousand miles on it and moved up to my next car. In fact, I got a new car every two or three years. I had credit cards and cash in my wallet, but I didn't spend the cash. I'd put everything on my cards and at the end of the month I'd make the minimum payments. I had grown up extremely poor as a kid. Now I was making up for it.

This went on for more than twenty years. That's why, when I got into the comedy business, I was as broke as I'd been when I was a teenager. I had a car, but I'd trade up all the time. I had an apartment, but I was paying rent and had never invested in a house. I had a little cash and a wallet full of credit cards but no savings.

There had to be a better way. This was the epiphany that happened to me, and until now I've told it only to several close friends.

Around 1983, clubs started to open beyond where I was near Atlanta. A couple of the first places I could work were Bruce Ayers's Comedy Club in Birmingham, Alabama (which he renamed the Stardome in 1994) and the Punchline in Columbia, South Carolina. I was still mostly an opening act. I didn't have enough money to get my car repaired, so I had to borrow my dad's pickup truck and borrow a hundred dollars from my brother to get there. One day in the summer, I was sitting at the picnic table in my parents' backyard. I was out there most of the time because I wanted to smoke. It hit me. I was thirty-six years old. I'd been working since I was twelve. And I started to cry. I'd been working for twenty-four years and what did I have to show for it? Nothing.

At that moment, I set a goal for myself. All the determination I had was going to be pointed toward meeting that goal. It wouldn't be a dream because dreams aren't real. I swore to make it a reality: I would never be broke again!

My true goal, my highest goal, would not be to get on *The Tonight Show*. It would not be to get on HBO. Those would be nice things to have and I wanted them, but I would not let those interfere with the purpose I'd set for my life, never to find myself in this situation again. I would be able to provide for myself, and I would never let my life go any other way for any reason.

I realized that I had to be serious about my career. Now, in my folks' backyard, I realized that I had to match my new outlook with a goal. A dream is never enough. You have to have a goal, and a goal requires a plan, starting with my finances, because if you can't pay your way in this world, you can't do anything else. I resolved that I would save 20 percent of everything I made. If I got a check for $600, I'd take $120 in cash and put it in my sock drawer at my parents' house.

From that time forward, I carried out my plan. Before I spent a penny, I paid myself first so I could provide for myself, and so I could be ready for the future, whatever came.

I put out my cigarette and went back in the house to see my mom. I had something to tell her. My parents were renting this house. They'd always rented, and they had not exactly been living in luxury. They'd never had carpet on the floor. They'd never had a house with central heat and air. Mom was standing over the stove, sweating in the summer heat. The only relief was an open window and a box fan across the room, and neither was making a dent in things.

I put my arm around my mother, and I said, "Mama, I think this comedy thing is going to work out. And when it does, I'm gonna buy you and Daddy a new house."

She said, "We're just fine. You just worry about yourself."

But what she didn't know is that I had made up my mind. This "comedy thing"—and all that would come with it—wasn't a dream anymore. It was my goal, and I was going to get there, and that was a certainty.

You can divide my life into two phases, before this day and everything after. I didn't want to be poor anymore, and now I had a plan to make it come true. This changed everything.

That happened in 1983. Four years later, I had accumulated enough cash in that drawer for a down payment on a house. When I was ready to make the purchase, I carried that cash down to the bank, but they wouldn't take it. I figured a "cash down payment" meant paper money. I was wrong. They asked me to open an account and put the money in there first, so that's what I did.

That house I bought? It was for my parents. Two months later, I bought one for myself.

Here's the Story: Two Million Acres for an Owl?

"As a layman, here's what I know: when it comes to the human species, two full-sized adults can mate in the back seat of a Honda Civic."

The way I tell it is pretty much the way I came up with it. I read this in the newspaper, or maybe I saw it on the news. Probably a little of both.

Out in California, they were expanding a major highway. They had spent $70 million when they realized that the highway was headed directly through the nesting area of some kind of rat, and that rat was an endangered species. They had to abandon everything they'd done, reroute the construction, and lose the $70 million, which as I say in the story, I really do think is ridiculous. To make it funnier, I bumped up the cost and changed five thousand acres to a couple million. I put this story with one about the spotted owl and it fit together just right.

YOU HAVE TO BE YOUR OWN BOSS

Since those days, everything I have ever owned has been paid for by the fans of stand-up comedy. The most important people in the theater or the nightclub or wherever I'm performing are not the entertainers on the stage. It's the people in the audience. Without them—without you—there'd be no show.

You may think if comedians don't show up, there's no show, but that's not quite it. If the audience doesn't show up, there's no reason for the comedians to be there at all. This is what I try to tell comedians. The sooner they understand this, the better their lives are going to be.

The audience is what a lot of us call "civilians"—in other words, normal people—and that's a very good thing to be. They're mechanics, plumbers, truck drivers, office workers, secretaries, receptionists, they work at the bank, they work in restaurants, but whatever they do, they work hard for the money and they're spending some of that money to see you. Those are the men and women paying my bills—and if you're in show business, they're paying yours, too. I figured that out thirty years ago and I still believe that today.

Just like someone with a garage or a sandwich shop, a comedian is self-employed. We pay mortgages. We have to feed our families. If you're a mechanic or a sandwich maker out on your own, you can't show up to do what you do and treat it like a joke. Neither can a comedian. If you can't tell the difference between telling a joke and treating your job like a joke, you won't be doing any job for long. It's hard to get entertainers into that mindset, and a lot of them can't get there at all. Reality has to make it for them.

I had taken myself off one path and put myself onto another. I decided to quit chasing a "dream." That's because a dream is just a nice, vague thought about what might be fun to have. Instead, I set a well-defined goal for myself, to be a professional comedian who supports himself by doing stand-up comedy in nightclubs and theaters. With that goal in mind, I then created a plan and took steps to become a professional entertainer, and to build a long-term career. All that required a lot of choosing between one thing and another, saying yes to some things and no to others, and making a lot of difficult decisions. I made every one of those decisions with my goal in mind, to be able to support myself as a comedian. Being focused like that made me different from a lot of comedians.

One of the most important decisions I made was that I wouldn't appear on stage unless I was paid to be there. I was just getting started, so it's not like people were going, *Oh, look! It's James Gregory!* But that's the point. If you're on stage too much, you very quickly give people the idea that you're "just a local." If you do a lot of guest sets, they can see you for free a few times a month. Those people aren't gonna wanna pay twenty-five or thirty dollars to see you next time you're there.

I was just getting started in Atlanta. My home club was the Punchline, but I would stay away from the club unless I was booked to perform. When my comedian friends were working, I would come in the back door and watch their shows from the sound booth. When the audience was gone, I would come down and hang out with my friends. The audience never knew I was there.

Comedians are entertainers at heart. We love the spotlight. And a lot of comedians, no matter how popular they are, will go on stage every chance they get. My goal was to become a paid performer who made his entire living doing comedy. I needed to be a performer who was worth going out of your way to see, one you couldn't see just anytime. So I stopped giving away my show. It was a calculated business decision and it paid off.

RESPECT

I admire many comedians, and by "admire" I also mean "respect," because it's a demanding job that deserves respect. When I talk about a stand-up, I'm always going to use the word "comedian."

This is something Ritch Shydner and I have talked about. Ritch is a hilarious comedian, the kind other comedians admire and want to be like. (He's been kind enough to say some nice things about me, too. It means a lot, coming from someone as good at this as he is. You can read his story in his book, *Kicking Through the Ashes*.) When I was getting started, he was already a talented professional and one of the hottest acts on the circuit. Ritch was and is the guy everyone wanted to see, especially other comedians. I tell young comedians to look him up on YouTube and just watch, because they'll learn a lot about comedy from the experience.

In 1993, I had an office across the parking lot from the Punchline where he was working. He would come into my office and we'd spend the afternoon just talking. One of the things that came up is something I'll always remember, something we agreed was important, something that is important to me to this day: I'm never going to use the word "comic." Except for this chapter, the word "comic" does not appear in this book. I don't like the word and I never use it. I didn't hear it much at all until the 1980s. In the

1980s, comedians became "comics." Used cars became "preowned vehicles." And heartburn became "acid reflux disease."

I say "comedian," and I'm pretty strict about it. I think that's because of what I associate with the word. When I was a kid, I looked forward to reading the Sunday funny papers so, to me, a "comic" is a color cartoon like Beetle Bailey. That's a different thing entirely. I've even corrected people on the radio. They'll said, "You've been a comic for—" and I'll cut in to say, "I'm not a comic. I'm a comedian."

I'm not the only one who feels this way. In the thirty years Johnny Carson was the host of *The Tonight Show*, he introduced over a thousand comedians to America, a lot of them for the very first time on TV. He never, never, never used the word "comic." David Letterman was the same way on his show. He respected the performer and the skill, and he always said "comedian," not "comic."

Another comedian I want to single out is Jeff Foxworthy. Jeff and I have only spoken once or twice over the past thirty years., but nearly forty years ago during our struggling, starving years, we hung out a lot at the Punchline in Atlanta, and we occasionally worked together.

After the show, and more than likely after watching someone else's show, we would go across the street to the IHOP or Waffle House to get a bite to eat, to talk about comedy, and to wonder what kind of future might lie ahead.

In one of those conversations at the Waffle House, Jeff said "I just don't want to end up being another comic at the bar." He and I both understood that early on: we didn't have just some dream. We had a goal. And Jeff reached that goal beyond imagination.

Because of their affiliation with Jeff—plus their own great talent and hard work toward a goal—a couple other comedians became successful multimillionaires. Ron White and Larry the Cable Guy are two of the funniest guys on the planet.

Jeff Foxworthy didn't just build a career; he built an empire. And my respect and admiration for him is never ending.

It's not just comedians who respect other comedians. As time goes on, you come to see how much respect other entertainers have for comedians. That's because this is not like any other kind of entertainment. It's one person with a microphone, and that's it. In fact, pretty much anybody in the public eye knows how difficult it is to do what we do.

There was this lady who had her own fundraiser for muscular dystrophy at the same time as the annual Jerry Lewis Labor Day telethon. Celebrities, athletes, and entertainers from around the country flew into Hilton Head to donate their time, but they weren't there to perform. Instead, wealthy people, what I call "money people," would fly in, too, and pay to play a round of golf with one of the stars, then attend a banquet. I was the entertainment for the evening, sharing the bill with the great Vince Gill. This nice lady had seen me perform at a comedy club in Savannah, Georgia, and she asked me to do my comedy for these five hundred generous people who had come out for a good cause and a good time.

By the way, when this took place back in 1987, one of the celebrities that night was the great songwriter Don Schlitz, who wrote "The Gambler." It was also the first time I sat down with Vince Gill, who was already on his way to becoming a country music legend. Vince went up early in the show and I was the closing act. As the years have gone by, I've said—as a joke, and not publicly, but just to friends—that Vince Gill was my opening act.

When the Sunday banquet was over, the organizers had set up a hospitality room for the celebrities. That's where I met the first man to walk on the moon, Neil Armstrong. After his career as an astronaut, he worked at lots of things but made a home at his farm in Ohio. He was a quiet, bashful guy who knew how to handle himself in front of a camera and an audience but by and large chose to stay out of the public eye.

He came up to me and said, "Oh, man! You're so funny! But how could you stay on stage and talk to five hundred strangers for an hour?"

"Well," I said, "it was just forty-five minutes."

"Whatever it is," he said, "I'd be scared to death."

"You scared? You walked on the moon!"

"True," he said, "but I only had to do it once. You guys do it every week."

Neil Armstrong walked on the moon, but he thought I was the brave one. Isn't that something?

DO YOU WANNA BE FAMOUS FOR NOW, OR SUCCESSFUL FROM NOW ON?

"Would you like to be on *The Tonight Show*?"

That's what Fred de Cordova asked me. He was the executive producer of *The Tonight Show With Johnny Carson*, and he'd been at the Hilton Head show, too. Would I like to be on the Carson show? Of course! I told him I'd love to. He gave me his phone number and said he'd set me up with Jim McCawley. That's a name that no one in the audience would know but if you were a comedian, you for sure knew. Jim was Carson's guy who picked the comedians. If you wanted to get on the show, and of course every comedian did, you had to make Jim McCawley happy.

As I was writing this book, it occurred to me that there's something that's been forgotten over the years, something I have to mention so you can better understand how important this story is. Late-night TV is a major destination for comedians. There's Kimmel, Colbert, Fallon, and before that, others that came and went, most importantly David Letterman. These days, there are lots of other chances for comedians to get on TV besides late night, too: lots of daytime shows, syndicated talk shows, sketch comedy shows, and then there are podcasts and YouTube and a lot more. Any of those things can be good for your career, but they probably won't "make" you, not even Kimmel or Fallon.

But up until 1989, there was only one late-night show, Carson's *Tonight Show*. There simply weren't any other shows at that hour. Even Letterman was more of a niche audience, and he ran after Carson and wrapped up in the middle of the night. If you got on Carson, and if you played your cards right, you could enter the upper reaches of the comedy business, and maybe even show business over all: movies, TV, everything.

All that to say that you need to understand: getting on the Johnny Carson show was the most important opportunity any comedian could have. Nothing compared, absolutely nothing. In fact, if you couldn't get booked on *The Tonight Show*, you were going to have to find another way to make a career. For a comedian, this was almost the only path into television. A shot on *Carson* could literally change your life—if you could get it at all, and if you made the most of it once you got it.

So when I tell you that Fred de Cordova asked me if I might like to do the show, you have to consider how the comedy business worked then, which was much different from today. This was like winning the lottery. This was Willy Wonka's golden ticket. Few comedians even got invited to audition, much less actually get on the show. My time had come.

It was several months later that I finally got the courage to call up Fred in California. I assumed that this number would be his office and that a secretary or an assistant would pick up, but no. The man answered his own phone! I told him who I was and he said of course he remembered me. He wanted me to do a set the following Thursday night at the Improv in Los Angeles. He would make sure that Jim was there to see me.

As promised, Jim came out. After my performance, we talked. He was very nice, but he told me to come back in six months. "You need to speed up your cadence," he said.

Since you're reading this book, you've probably seen me perform, and you know that talkin' fast is not what I do. But this was *The Tonight Show* and all that it could bring, and Jim was only making one request. He hadn't criticized my material or my personality, just my speed. I decided that for this huge opportunity, that was something I was willing to do. In the shows that followed, I practiced speeding up my delivery a bit. Six months later, as instructed, I came back. Jim watched my show again, now with the changes. One more time, he told me to come back in another six months. Not what I expected.

I had to make a decision. Was he really interested in seeing me one more time, or was he just doing this to make Fred de Cordova happy? If I went even faster it wouldn't be just changing my speed anymore. It'd be about a different way to perform, and it didn't make sense to me to change my entire persona and my entire style just to get six minutes on television, even for the biggest opportunity in the comedy business, a set on *The Tonight Show*. To make a decision like that, to turn down *The Tonight Show*, I had to be dead certain of what I really wanted out of this career. By this time, I was.

This was my thinking. I knew already that I was good at what I do. If that wasn't what they wanted, if that wasn't good enough for them, then they didn't want my comedy. They wanted something else. I'd been through this before. I had already auditioned for the David Letterman show. The guy who booked Letterman had seen me perform in Asheville, North Carolina, and he had already told my manager, "David Letterman's not gonna like him." It wasn't that

Dave wouldn't "like" me, though. It was because they were looking for performers who fit with the host, and that was true whether it was Carson or Letterman. They wanted someone who delivered material and got the laugh on the basis of the material. A guy like me, where the laugh depended a lot on how I delivered it? They were never going to go for that. With James Gregory, you know what you're getting. There's no need for me to show you what you already know. It ain't gonna change. At that point, I made a decision that I would never audition again for a show, would never do a showcase to get work as a comedian. And I never did.

Jim McCawley was very gracious to me. I remember he told me that a set on *The Tonight Show* needed to be four and a half to five and a half minutes. I told Jim I needed three minutes just to clear my throat. And they were not asking for changes because of my accent or because they saw me as only a Southern act. Jeff Foxworthy was on the show in 1990, and Jeff's a Southern fella for sure. So why didn't McCawley book me? The same reason as with the Letterman show. You can talk all day long about how fast or slow you talk, what kind of material you do, and so on, but there's really only one test: does this comedian "fit" the host? Either you do or you don't, and that's completely up to the guy making the decision. In this case, it was Jim McCawley. He didn't think I was a fit. He was generous enough to offer to let me come back and try again, but I knew good and well that this was a basic thing about who I am and what I do. I could come back a dozen times and that wouldn't change. So I told him thanks, but no.

As important as the show was at the time, I've never regretted my decision. I'm explaining the details here because people who come to see me often wonder why my career doesn't include Carson and Letterman. Would it have made me a "big star"? It did that for a lot of people, especially getting *The Tonight Show* in the

1980s: Ray Romano, Roseanne Barr, and even David Letterman himself. Some of those comedians saw their lives change the very next day. You hoped that getting on the show would help you but there was no guarantee, of course. And I can give you a list of names who went on *The Tonight Show* and didn't make it, people who dropped out of the business or never got a bump in pay or popularity. A few people worked hard to get it and never did, then got it when they didn't need it anymore. Tim Allen did all the showcases and auditions for McCawley but he didn't get *The Tonight Show* until around the time he got the series *Home Improvement*. He was and is a very funny performer and a wonderful actor. The producers just didn't think he fit in.

So now you see why I was going to have to change in order to get on, and why I refused to do it. You may think that was a sacrifice, but it wasn't at all. In the sales business, the guy that hired me when I was twenty-five years old, a man named Mike Wilson, told me that there's always an Option A and Option B, but that there's no such thing as Option C, D, E, F, G, and H. Those are excuses and barriers. Option A and Option B are pretty simple: either you're going to do something or not. Either you're gonna pursue your goal or go after something else. The "Hollywood" dream that attracts so many entertainers is a very different thing from the goal of making a living as a performer. Over the years, I've seen lots of comedians who got to do a Letterman or a Carson or, later, Leno, Kimmel, and Fallon. Some of them did those shows several times. But many of them were back to struggling right after. They achieved their dream of being on TV, but it turned out that had little to do with becoming a professional who works consistently.

When Jim McCawley told me to come back in another six months, that experience from my sales days was heavy on my mind, and I put this thing in terms I'd learned years ago. There was Option A: I could become a professional dream chaser. There was also Option B: I could become a very successful professional entertainer. I chose Option B.

It proved to be the right choice. Television doesn't benefit comedians the way it used to, and that's a good thing. Used to be that you had to wait for Carson's people or, later, Letterman's people to come calling. And the variety shows—which aren't around anymore—were just for veteran comedians. These days those gatekeepers aren't nearly as important because there are other ways to get attention. You can put yourself on YouTube today and get nationwide attention literally tomorrow.

As for those late-night talk shows, I'm gonna go out on a limb and say their days are numbered. It's almost like what they call in retail, a "loss leader," meaning it costs more to put it out there than they make from it. Kimmel and Fallon are more like figure-heads for the network than big-draw entertainers. The host of Fox News's late-night comedy talk show, Greg Gutfeld, often has a bigger audience than *The Tonight Show*.

Like I said, I'm glad I chose Option B.

Here's the Story: The Miracle of Plywood

"We get some plywood, we can ride it out!"

I've lived my whole life in the South so, as I say sometimes when I'm on stage, I've seen the worst Mother Nature can throw at us.

A couple things got me thinking about what led to my story about people staying around during tornadoes when they ought to know better. One thing that put this story in my mind might have been the hurricane of 1992, the year Bill Clinton was campaigning against President George H. W. Bush. There'd been big storms in Florida. Clinton went to see the damage, but for some reason, President Bush didn't go. That was all over the news for a while. Another thing was something I've seen on TV over and over for years and years.

A storm will be coming and a reporter will go out to find someone to interview. A lot of times it's a couple on the way into Lowe's or Home Depot. They're not getting out of town before the storm. They're staying! And how are they going to survive? Why, they're going get some plywood. By the afternoon there are gonna be cars flying through the air, but these two are thinking, "A sheet of plywood, that'll protect us!" This couple's talking to the reporter while in the background you see army trucks, state police, and helicopters hustling everybody out of town. What were these two thinking, that everybody else couldn't find any plywood?

I figured they'd stay until the plywood sold out.

THREE MEN WHO
CHANGED MY LIFE

It takes a lot of experience to see things simply in a complicated situation. Somebody asks you if you want to be on *The Tonight Show* and tells you that all you have to do is to keep changing yourself a little more and wait just a little longer. That's tempting. If you don't know what you want, what you really want, you're going to make the wrong decision. To deal with an opportunity and a temptation like that, you have to condition yourself to think clearly before you get there. For me, it was that, and you have whatever it is for you. Whatever the case, the answer begins with knowing what you want in your life, being responsible for yourself, and making the decision to make your own choices.

There's always someone in your life who helps you figure out that sort of thing. I've long said that in my life, there have been three men who did that for me. If I'd received guidance from them and no one else, I still would have had a successful life. That's how important they were to me. They are my father, Mr. I. D. Reese, and Mr. Mike Wilson.

When I was in sales, I'd sit down with potential buyers and spend an hour or an hour and a half making my pitch. At the end,

I'd ask them to sign a contract, but that didn't guarantee the sale. The next step was to wait three days to find out if their credit had been approved. One week I wrote five contracts and three got turned down. I went into Mike Wilson's office to complain. He was my boss at the time, and he taught me about PAD.

I had written five contracts and three of them weren't approved. I was upset and angry. "I worked hard," I said. "Why doesn't that show in my paycheck? It's hard when you're working hard for nothing."

"For nothing?" he said. Mike took out a hundred-dollar bill and picked up a lighter. He then calmly set fire to that bill. I was only twenty-five years old. I was shocked. To Mike it probably looked like I was having a seizure.

We sat there watching it burn down to nothing in the big ashtray.

"James, that's just money," he said. "That's nothing more than a piece of paper." I wasn't so sure about that, but I kept listening. "You know how come I can burn that and not worry about it? Because I can make all the money I want. I'm gonna make some more tomorrow. I'll make some more today. I'm not on salary. I don't work in a job for a big company. I can make as much as I want to make—if I'm willing to work for it."

I was beginning to see: you can rely on what somebody else gives you for doing the minimum work they ask, or you can rely on yourself and the sky's the limit. The only thing stopping you is how hard you're willing to work.

"Instead of seeing ten prospects in a week," he said, "you see twelve. Instead of working forty hours a week, you work sixty. That's persistence, attitude, and determination. I call that PAD. If you've got that, you don't have to worry about money."

"You're writing your own paycheck, you see? That means you're bitching about the wrong things." He pointed to the ashes of the money. "I burned that bill, you see, but I can get as many more as I want. You can, too. So get your head out of your ass."

I did. I started making great money. Pretty soon I had a wallet full of cash. Though I didn't feel the need to set fire to any of it, Mr. Wilson showed me that I could, if I decided to be in charge of my own income and my own life.

***

I worked for Mr. I. D. Reese starting when I was eleven. He had a tiny store about as big as a good-sized carport, plus he had two gas pumps out front. It wasn't like it is today where you pay for how much you want and it stops. In those days, pumps were mechanical. They had gears inside that would spin around and show you the gallons and the price. Gas was about thirty cents a gallon, so five dollars bought you a lot of gas.

This wasn't a place where strangers dropped in. Mr. Reese knew everybody and everybody knew him. Most people would come in, leave their money on the counter, then shout into the back, "Hey, Reese! I'll have five dollars' worth of gas!" Then they'd go pump five dollars, down to the cent, and that was how it went. Once in a while, though, somebody would pump a little more, maybe on purpose, maybe not. But all it took was being a penny over and Mr. Reese would come shouting out of the back.

"Hey! Come back here! You owe me a penny!" I was a kid and I thought that was so mean. One day it happened and I said what I was thinking. "Mr. Reese, it's only a penny." I didn't have to wait long to get an answer.

"Junior," he said—nobody called me James until I was a grown man—"I've been here twenty-five years. If just once—just one time—in those twenty-five years, somebody had pumped $4.99 and said, 'Hey Reese, I left you five dollars,' you might have a point."

I didn't understand what he meant, and I told him. And he told me what I still didn't understand.

"When somebody says *it's just a penny*, they're always talking about somebody else's penny," he said, "and it's probably *your* penny. But when it's *their* penny, it's a whole different story." He was teaching me a lesson I'd need to know for the rest of my life, a lesson I'd live by: you have to look out for your own money and you have to look out for yourself. "If they were giving me an extra penny, then I'd be fine giving somebody else a penny once in a while, but that never happens."

"If it's just a penny," he said, "it's my penny." He didn't mince words. He understood that you have to look out for yourself, and he taught me that as clearly as such a thing could be taught. To this day, I have a placard in my home in his honor.

***

Mr. Reese taught me useful things by telling me exactly what he was thinking. My dad was different. He never lectured us kids. He wasn't a highly educated man. He made it to the fourth grade. My mother made it to the third. We were very poor, on and off welfare a few times. At Christmas time we'd get used toys that a church had donated.

But I heard him say so many times growing up, just like Mr. Reese, nobody owes you anything. Same lesson, just learned from the other side. Mr. Reese knew that people look out for themselves first, 'cause he'd seen it even with a penny at the pump. My dad knew that people look out for themselves first because when you don't have much, you have to go get what you want on your own. Nobody's gonna walk over and give it to you. Dad knew that counting on charity, or kindness if you wanna call it that, was not a secure way to live. It was rough, but that's how poverty is.

Also, my father was an alcoholic, and his father before him. My dad was one of three brothers—making them my uncles, of course—and two sisters, my aunts. All the men had this alcohol problem, too. My dad's mother died when he was fourteen. That's when he started drinking. Also at that time, the state took the girls away. My dad wouldn't see them again for fifteen or twenty years.

So at age fourteen, my dad had to go to work in north Georgia in just about the only job he could get at that time and at that age, driving a sawmill truck—I'm not joking with you. He drove a logging truck with an open cab, no top, and a long truck bed that carried the trunks of trees. He was driving those trucks and drinking, working just to feed the rest of the family and survive. He was twenty-one when he married my mother. She was sixteen.

The drinking went on for years, and it was still heavy when I was a boy. My dad and his brothers didn't go to nightclubs. They'd drink at home, and drink homemade liquor. The fact that Dad even survived all this, and that he and Mom raised us in all this? That's a miracle all by itself.

So all the years of alcoholism and the poverty, they weren't easy. But maybe knowing that can help you understand why I believe so strongly, with all my heart, that you have to do what you have to do to survive. It's your responsibility, nobody else's. If you're waiting for help to come, you're gonna be waiting a long time. Oh, it might come, but you can't guarantee anything except what you do yourself.

I learned that by living it and watching—I just observed how my dad chose to live, and he never lectured anybody. I saw what worked and what didn't, of course. I also saw things that have nothing to do with money or poverty and everything to do with what kind of man you ought to be.

For example, my sister passed away in 2019 at the age of seventy-seven. In a lifetime, my sister never heard me use a curse word. That's not by accident. That's very much on purpose. See, I cuss all the time. I have a foul mouth. We'd be at my parents' house, out in the back on a Sunday, me and my brother, my brother-in-law, my dad, probably a neighbor or two, and we all used cuss words. (Though my dad never used the F-word. He'd for sure want me to mention that here.) I remember my dad talking about the next day, and my brother saying that tomorrow was *mother-effing Monday*. Across the yard was the back of the house, of course, and a sliding screen door into the kitchen. That's where my mother and my sister were. I could say those words in the yard but I knew I was never to use those words in front of my sister or my mother. If I did, I'd be a dead man, Dad would see to that. That's why I've always had this rule about watching my mouth. You can say *damn, hell,* or *I don't give a shit,* little things like that, mild things in front of a lady. But *eff this* and *gee-dee that* and worse—God help you if you talked that way in front of a female. On that one, God wasn't gonna save me or anybody else from my dad.

He taught me to show special respect for women. The county came by and picked up the trash every Wednesday where we lived on Old Covington Road. The night before, one of us boys would take the trash out to the road. That's because of Dad's rule, and this was word for word: "Don't ever, ever let a woman be seen totin' trash. That's not a woman's job. That's a man's job." In our house, my mom worked hard. She cooked, she cleaned, she washed the clothes. We respected that work and it was all inside. Letting the public see a woman reduced to doing work outside, heavy lifting of a trash barrel? That was and is disrespectful.

Some people call that sexist, but they're the ones with the problem, not me. That's not sexism. That's showing respect. I'll never in my life apologize for being respectful to women, or to anybody else who deserves respect. Respect is important. That's always gonna be true. Now whether people wanna live that way or not? That's a different story. Dignity toward yourself. Dignity for others. You don't really learn that in a classroom or in college. You learn it from the people around you if you're lucky enough to have those kinds of people in your life. You learn that by example.

That's not to say that my daddy's example was perfect. Oh, no. I've been pretty clear he was far from perfect. There were always threats of divorce and more, usually due to a lack of money or lack of food. But he was a good man at heart, and he tried to live that way even if he didn't always succeed. Who does?

FAITH

I do believe in God. I don't make a big deal about it, don't preach about it, don't lecture other people. But I know what I believe. When I was a boy, most Sundays I went to Sunday school. My dad would go to church occasionally but not too often. We went to a little church in the country. There were some good folks there and I benefited from how good they were.

You'll often hear someone look back on a childhood like mine and say, "We were poor but we didn't know it." I damn well knew it! We were poor enough that once in a while we went hungry. We had neighbors who might figure that out and they'd bring us extra food. Or somebody at the church would realize we were having a problem and somebody there would bring a basket of groceries and leave it at the door.

I'm sure there are still churches like that here and there where the concern is looking out for one another and those in need, but the church that I used to know is not the church I see today. For instance, I think megachurches ought to be taxed. A lot of them don't even look like church buildings. They're concert halls, the kinds of places I perform, and what goes on looks a lot like a show, right down to having to buy a ticket to get in. As somebody in show business, I can tell you that I pay taxes. Kenny Chesney pays taxes. Bruce Springsteen pays taxes. We're all in the entertainment business. Some of these preachers are also in the entertainment business, but they don't pay taxes. Oh, they have huge mansions, a couple extra homes, and a fleet of automobiles. A few have their own airports plus helicopters and jets, and real estate like strip centers and office buildings. These are the kinds of things that really wealthy entertainers might have—and pay taxes on. But in this case, all that stuff is titled to the church so it doesn't get taxed. That's not religion. That's a hustle. Now, I respect a hustle, but I don't respect pretending like it's something else. Maybe I could save some money and be Reverend James Gregory.

My relationship with God is good. I can talk to Him anytime I want to. I don't have to go down at 9 a.m. every Sunday to make sure I'm in line with my ticket. God can hear me if I want to talk to Him, sitting on my couch having a cup of coffee. That's the way I believe.

Do not doubt it: God has given me a reason to believe He's up there. Here's why.

***

My dad was a cigar smoker—well, he probably chewed on it more than he smoked. He'd smoke a Tampa Cub or a Tampa Nugget. They were a nickel apiece. But there were also Dutch Masters, and they were fifteen cents. A pack of five Tampa Cubs was a quarter, but a pack of Dutch Masters was seventy-five cents—big difference, in those days. If my dad had what he would call a good week, he'd splurge and treat himself to Dutch Masters. Those kinds of weeks didn't come too often so he didn't smoke Dutch Masters on a regular basis, just when he had a little bit of money, when things were going pretty good for a bit. I tell you that so I can tell you this.

In 2004, I had quadruple bypass surgery. On June 16, my sister's birthday, I went to sleep at 6:30 in the morning. I woke up July 18, over thirty days later. For that month, I was in a medically induced coma. They almost lost me.

I was supposed to be under for five and a half to six hours. When I woke up, as far as I was concerned, that's how long it had been. I didn't know I'd been out for thirty-two days. I couldn't talk because I had a tracheotomy in my throat to let me breathe. Besides that, when you've been in that position for a month, you can't talk anyway. I was trying to say something but I couldn't. The nurse gave me a legal pad and a Sharpie. I wrote on the legal pad, *Where's Daddy?* My sister gave me a strange look, because my father had passed away nearly ten years before. Finally, she said, "He couldn't be here today." Later that night, she told me that I'd been out for so long in a coma. By this time, I could mumble a few words, and I said, *Well, Daddy was here.*

I knew he'd been there because, when I woke up, I could smell Dutch Masters cigars.

I told the staff. They thought I was crazy. "Don't you smell it?" I said. Of course they said they couldn't smell anything. The next day it wasn't as strong but it was still there and I asked them again, "Can you smell cigar smoke? 'Cause I do." This went on for a couple of days, strong smell of cigar smoke. They never smelled it but I sure did.

I remember that room, of course. It had a TV and side chair, plus a bigger chair with an ottoman. To this day, I believe that my dad sat in that chair. I believe he sat there until I woke up, and only then did he leave. He sat there in that chair to make sure his boy survived. That's what I believe.

Now, here's the kicker.

I love ice cream. In fact, I believe there's no such thing as bad ice cream. I've always been a vanilla person. It's the best flavor. I add things to it like crushed pineapple, melted chocolate, crumbled-up Oreos or chocolate-chip cookies, fresh strawberries, but always vanilla for the ice cream, always and to this day. My daddy loved butter pecan, and that's all he ate. As he got older, got a decent job, my mother kept ice cream in the freezer because Dad liked to have a little bit of ice cream every night of his life.

On my fourth or fifth day in the hospital, I couldn't eat anything solid, just broth, Jell-O, mashed potatoes, things like that. My sister asked if I wanted some vanilla ice cream.

"No, I don't," I said. "Go down there and get me some butter pecan."

She looked at me. "What do you mean? You always get vanilla."

"No, I don't," I said. "If you're going down there, get me some butter pecan."

It was so intense and I feel it so strong today, it almost makes me cry. My sister has told this story for years—she remembers it as well as I do. I was mad about that ice cream, and I was convinced that I always had butter pecan.

I believe that was my dad. I believe it with my heart and soul. I believe my father was in that hospital the whole time I was there. That comes from a higher power. It doesn't really matter if anybody else believes it. That's what I believe.

***

There are so many things in the world you can't explain. You might want to be an atheist but when push comes to shove, it's hard to stick with it. We've all heard stories about bedside miracles. I love pro wrestling, especially the old-school wrestlers themselves. One of the most famous wrestling families was the Von Erich family. One of the sons was wrestling overseas and injured his shoulder to the point he needed surgery. Shouldn't have been any big deal, right? Well, he came out of surgery and ended up with what they called toxic shock syndrome. His temperature spiked. Doctors couldn't bring it down. He wasn't getting enough oxygen, either. The doctors didn't have much hope for his survival. One of the doctors came out to the waiting room to tell the family that if they wanted to see the boy, they'd better do it now, because it didn't look like he was going to make it. Their minister was there and he said that before they go in, they should pray. And that's what they did.

Before they were finished, the doctor came back out with that look in his face, and you know the look I'm talking about. "His temperature went down," he said. The doctor told them their boy was going to pull through. That little miracle happened in less than a minute, right after the doctor told them to tell him goodbye.

Somebody else is in charge. That's what I believe.

Besides, I don't have the courage to not believe. I heard a story once about a couple fellas went to high school and college together, knew each other forever. The whole time the one guy would make fun of anybody who was religious or even believed in God. "That's the same people who believe in the Easter Bunny and Santa Claus," he'd say.

Over the years, they stayed close but they would debate, always about "hypothetical" this and "hypothetical" that. Finally, the guy came up with this. "Let me ask you another hypothetical thing," he said. "You have an eight-year-old, healthy, beautiful little girl. That's as real as real can be. Let's say, hypothetically, like you always say, that you and your family are gathered in the ICU because of some tragic accident. The doctors have told you that your little girl has only 50 percent chance to make it through the night. Now, hypothetically speaking, as a man who doesn't believe in God. Would you want me to pray for your little girl?"

He didn't hesitate. "Absolutely," he said.

The other one said, "Then you're not really an atheist."

I like that story. I don't have it all figured out, but the good news is I don't have to. Neither do you. All you have to do is believe.

THE FUNNIEST MAN IN AMERICA

ost of my career I've been known as the Funniest Man in America. You might think I came up with that myself, but that's not the case at all. How that name came to be? Purely accidental.

It started in Huntsville, when I was working a club there very early on, in the mid-1980s. There was and still is a newspaper there called the *Huntsville Times*. Now keep in mind, in the 1980s, the newspaper was the main way you'd communicate with the public and get your news. Well, a guy named Billy Joe Cooley had a column in that paper twice a week where he'd write about the shows he'd seen—not comedy shows, 'cause they didn't have any—but everything else, plays at the high school, movies, the band doing cover songs at the local lounge. He did this for years.

Comedy clubs were new, of course, and the one in Huntsville hadn't been open for very long. I did not know this, but Billy Joe Cooley was in the audience for my Wednesday night show. On Friday he had an article about his first visit to a comedy club. It wasn't a story about me, just about the experience he had at the show. But as part of the story, he wrote something that would become a part of what I do for the rest of my life. He said that the headliner was a guy named James Gregory and that this fellow had to be the "funniest man in America."

It is impossible to overstate just how valuable this was for me. In the 1980s, long before the internet, newspapers were the only kind of widespread promotion you could have. As for credits, there weren't that many to have because there weren't that many clubs. If the comedian coming next week had a credit like *The Tonight Show* or *As Seen on HBO*, that was a big deal. A credit had to be New York or LA. I didn't have anything like that—until Billy Joe wrote what he wrote. "The Funniest Man in America"—now I had something to promote!

I knew what to do: I bought a bunch of copies, highlighted it, and put it in the front of my press kit with my headshot and bio. Then I mailed it out to clubs so they could promote me if I was coming there or consider hiring me if I hadn't been there yet.

My next stop was the Funny Bone comedy club in St. Louis, so I sent my new press kit there. It arrived before I did. When I walked in, the other two comedians on the show were already making fun of me, because in their newspaper in St. Louis, it said that appearing this weekend at the St. Louis Funny Bone would be "the funniest man in America." I was embarrassed, but not all that much. This was excellent publicity! When somebody says something that big about you, there's not much to do except make as much use of it as you can—and try to live up to it for the rest of your life.

For a while, people, especially other comedians, might say to me, "Don't you mean funniest man in Georgia? Or funniest man in the South? You sure it's the whole country?" Yep, I'm sure. Funniest man in America. I didn't ask for the title. It was awarded to me!

When I would go to the Funny Bone in St. Louis, I would also go to the ones in Texas because they own the Funny Bones in Dallas-Fort Worth and Arlington. They sent that quote to their other clubs. Pretty soon it was clear to me that this was an opportunity. I began to think that maybe I had something here with the "funniest man in America" stuff. It took guts to grab onto that claim, but I did it. I started putting it on everything: *James Gregory, Funniest Man in America.* It helped people remember me, gave me a brand, you might say. It's such a hook, such a draw, that there are people who know "Funniest Man in America" but don't know my name.

I was fortunate enough to have the foresight to have it trademarked. That means nobody can use that phrase to promote themselves but me. If Billy Joe Cooley hadn't written that story, calling myself that would never have occurred to me at all.

I've had moments when people would push back on it. One time I was in San Jose, an hour from San Francisco, which is of course the home to a lot of very funny acts. It was the first night of the week and I was telling the emcee how to introduce me: "The funniest man in America, James Gregory!"

"Are you sure you want to say that?" he said.

"I am," I said.

"You really want me to tell them you're the funniest man in America? David Letterman has been on this stage. Robin Williams has been on this stage. But *you*—you're the funniest man in America? Are you funnier than Robin Williams?"

"Son," I said, "just do it."

I get asked most often on the radio, but I'm ready for them. "How did you get to be the funniest man in America?" they'll ask.

"I had an advantage," I'll tell them. "I've been doing this so long that when I started, America was just thirteen states."

Here's the Story: A Conspiracy to Make Us Look Ignorant on TV

"Get out to the trailer park and interview a dumbass."

This is another story where I got the idea from what I've seen my whole life. Once again, this is about TV reporters and storms. This time, though, it's not about the interviews before the storm. This is about what happens after.

I challenge anyone to say they saw the news, local or national, where the reporter was out there interviewing someone who had lost their home, usually a mobile home—I challenge you to find any person they interview who doesn't look like an idiot. It's like they go looking for 'em. It's never somebody in a pair of good-looking slacks, never a dress shirt, or a suit, or a tie. Apparently the only people who lose their house in a tornado are rednecks. It's always a guy in a John Deere cap with a ring of keys on his belt, somebody wearing camo, or some lady with no teeth! These storms don't just happen in places where rednecks live, but somehow that's all these TV people can find to talk to. I think they do it on purpose.

WHERE THE FUNNY STUFF COMES FROM

When you are an entertainer, especially a comedian, having something catchy and memorable attached to you besides your name is very, very valuable. You want people to come see you over and over, and they need something to hang onto. "Funniest Man in America," FMIA, gives them a way to remember who you are and what they like about you.

Besides being known by that name, I've had various lines in my routines that people remember, things people like so well they walk up to me and say them. For a long time, I had this line: "It could be a law, I don't know." I'd use it as a callback, as we call it, something you say up front as part of a joke, then you say it again later to make another joke. That line was accidental, too! I didn't plan it. Here's how it happened. I used to do a routine about midgets, or little people as I think we're supposed to say these days. "We've all seen midgets," I'd say. "But it's always a midget with a full-sized girlfriend. You never see a whole midget family. You just don't! I don't know why. Maybe it's against the law." And that would set it up for me to pay off later. I'd do other material, then I'd come back. "Anytime you see a midget, they're married to a full-sized person. It could be a law. I don't know!"

That's how that line was born. Almost immediately I started using it in other places in my show. It's a natural thing comedians do once they start figuring out how to be funny.

When I first started doing comedy, I was like most people who go up for the first time, I knew what I thought was funny and that was about it. That's the easy part. What a comedian has to do is figure out what other people think is funny. What you usually do is start with what you think is funny to you and make it funny for everybody else. I had an advantage in connecting with people because I had worked in sales so many years, but selling is different from standing in front of an audience that came to laugh. I won't say I was bad when I first started doing comedy, but I did have a lot of times where I wasn't good.

What I had that made me unique was a way to make up for whatever was lacking: I could say things that weren't necessarily funny, but I had a presence on stage right away that allowed me to work things out and get away with not having a big joke because they liked the way I told it. When you're comfortable on stage, it makes the audience comfortable, and that gives you some leeway. I also had an advantage because I had been in sales for so long. I was comfortable connecting with people, especially with people who might doubt you right off. I definitely wasn't afraid to talk to strangers. When you're in sales, you have to talk to a total stranger for an hour and a half. So being in front of people didn't bother me, never did.

Besides trying out your stuff on open mic nights, which they didn't have when I started out, your first job in comedy is to be the emcee, or what's also known as the opener. When you first start the show, nobody's really paying attention to you. They're ordering their drinks and getting seated, getting comfortable. When you're the opening act it's hit and miss. But that changes tremendously once you get to the feature spot—not completely, but it gives you a chance to see what might work. What you thought wasn't funny as an opener? All of a sudden, it's funny because now you've got a little more time to do it right, the audience is a little more attentive, warmed up, and you've got time to do it right. You could tell that was the case even as an opener going up at the start of the evening versus going up with a little material between the feature and the headliner.

It's important to be able to come up with funny material, but what's most important is to be able to perform it. A famous agent was asked if he were going to sign someone on your roster, would it be someone you thought was a good writer, or someone who was a great performer. He said, ideally of course it would be both. But if he had to choose, it'd always be the performer. There used to be a line in my promotional material that someone said they thought I could read the phonebook out loud and make it funny. I might have to try that someday. But I like the fact that while some people say funny things, I can say things funny.

People ask me if I remember the first joke I ever told. No, I don't. I have no idea what it was. All I know for sure was that I was doing some of the things I did when I had been in sales, things that would put people at ease and make them laugh. One thing I do remember from early on was a thing about furniture polish. To this day, if you go to Kroger or Publix, there'll be a lemon pie there every time, and it'll say, "made with artificial lemon." Or get one of those Entenmann's desserts, the prebaked stuff. Same thing, it says artificial lemon. But go over three aisles to furniture polish and that stuff's made with real lemons! We're putting real lemon juice on the furniture, and we're eating the artificial stuff.

Another thing people ask is if I write all my own material. The answer is yes, I do. I have never bought material. People call my manager all the time and say they'd be a great writer for me but I won't do that because I'm not so sure what they come up with is theirs. It's easy to hear something and forget it, then a little while later to think you thought it up. So I don't want to take that risk. Besides, after all these years, I have plenty of material. That's not me saying I'm a great writer. I'm not a writer, not a guy who sits down at a desk. I know how to do what I do for the stage but I can't just wake up in the morning and take a legal pad and a pen and say, okay, I need to write some new stuff today. I admire people who can do that, but I can't do that. I have to hear something, see something, observe something I can embellish upon. And sometimes things just come to me. The first four or five years I made notes, but that was it. These days, I don't write anything down. I haven't written down something on a piece of paper in thirty-five years.

What I do on stage changes, of course. You learn how strong something is, and how to make it stronger and funnier, by performing it. There's no other way to find out. I add new material and take out old things. Other times I move things around. Some routines I keep in for years because I know the people who come to see me want to hear them again. For many years, I've had a routine about that one relative that everybody has, that "wide" relative, you might say, the "big" one. She's the one who puts on a show of her own after a big meal at the house. Like a lot of routines, it started out small but got bigger. As I added things, this one eventually stretched out to eight or nine minutes: "This is going to remind you of somebody you know. If they're no longer with you, it'll bring back good memories, maybe of your favorite aunt or your grandmother. If you didn't see 'em on Sunday, you'd see 'em on a special occasion—you know, Christmas Day, Thanksgiving, somebody's birthday...."

I'm talking about that one relative we all have, of course. The "wide" one—the big, friendly, overweight aunt or uncle or cousin. We love 'em so much, and after they have that big dinner, they wander into the living room, maybe unhook those britches or at least loosen that belt a notch or two to give yourself a little room to breathe. They rub their belly, lay their arms out, stretch their legs, make funny sounds, probably burp a few times...and then they start talking. I sit down in a chair and act that out, all the moves and the facial expressions and the things they say. You can imagine how that routine could start with one or two lines and grow into what it has become. By now that routine has over ten million views on YouTube and Facebook. More people have seen it there than have seen me do it live, and I've done it in person literally thousands of times.

When I started doing that routine, I did it in the middle of my show, but as the piece got longer, that became a problem because I couldn't top it! That's when I moved it to the end, to make it a "closer" bit, and that's where I kept it from then on. I learned that I couldn't follow the fat lady. That's one of the ways I develop material on stage, and I enjoy doing it that way, figuring it out at the same time as the audience enjoys it. But the stage is another place where it matters to have a goal and a plan. I would never go up to just talk and see what happens. But if you go up with an idea, maybe you know where you're headed with a story and how it's gonna wrap up, maybe you have a few funny things to say already or a place to end it—you can call that "writing on stage," maybe— but when you're up there, you're there to entertain people who paid for it, not to work out your act. If you're gonna improvise, be sure you can pay it off for the customers.

DO THEY ASK TAYLOR SWIFT THAT?

These days, most of the places where I perform are theaters. There are a lot of them around the country, and for the many dozens of theaters I visit, I'll do a show there about once a year. These places usually seat four hundred to a thousand people, and they're most often in small towns where they don't have comedy clubs. Turns out, theater shows are a somewhat new thing in comedy. Used to be that unless you lived in or near a good-size town with a comedy club, you didn't get to see live comedy. A lot of small towns have theaters that have been dormant for fifty years or more, but now they're being brought back, and they're booming. These theater shows let me bring my show to a lot of people who've heard of me but who have never seen me in person.

For instance, I play in Calhoun, Georgia, every year. There's a great theater there called the Gem Theatre. It has about five hundred seats. That's where this business about new material comes in. When I go back to a place a year after I've been there, do you really think that there's gonna be the exact same five hundred people sitting in the same chairs they sat in a year ago? Of course not. There'll be a percentage of the audience who have never seen me, another percentage who've seen me before, maybe that year or maybe long before. Out of those people, there's one type of person

I always hear from after the show. They want to be sure I know that I left out their favorite story!

When people come to see me, a lot of them want the "greatest hits." I'm happy to deliver! I'm proud that so many people like to hear my stories over and over again. They like new stuff, but they also like the old stuff, too, and I deliver that, like a band might play the greatest hits. They're my customers—you are my customers. I go on stage and give the people what they want. That's my job! I add new material all the time, but some stories I know you want to hear again.

Some comedians are always worried about repeating themselves. I've heard so many of them say, "I was here just three months ago. I better put in a bunch of new stuff." I don't think it's necessary, at least not as necessary as they might think.

Not long ago, a reporter for a paper in North Carolina asked and I tried to answer in a very polite way. "Are you gonna do a new show this time, or the same as last time?" he said.

I interrupted. "Before I get to your question, lemme ask you one. You've interviewed a lot of entertainers over the years, I'm sure. When you are interviewing Kenny Chesney, Taylor Swift, or any other singer, do you say to them, *You were just here a year ago. Are you gonna do the same old songs, or do you have a bunch of new ones?*"

One evening, I was between shows at Comedy Off Broadway, Jeff Gilstrap's club in Lexington, Kentucky. Jeff passed away over a decade ago, but he was always my friend and will always be one of my all-time favorite people. On this particular night, he was telling a story on me—rather, about all of you who come to see my shows. "Sometimes it's a little crazy," he said.

Someone called who had seen me just a few months before. He asked Jeff if I was gonna do the same material or something new. Jeff told the guy, "It's the same old shit!" I thought that was pretty funny, but then Jeff gave the best punchline of all.

The caller said, "Great! I'll take six tickets!"

COMEDY IS GOOD FOR YOU!

I believe strongly that people need to laugh. It's more than liking funny stories. Our bodies need it. I think our souls need it, too. I really do believe that. There was a writer named Norman Cousins who proved it's true, as far as I'm concerned.

He wrote books and magazine articles for many years. He did something else, too, and it was a lot different from writing. He became a professor who taught in the department of psychiatry at the University of California. Eventually, he did research on the connection between laughter and the body's ability to fight illness. That's where his story gets interesting.

In 1964, he was diagnosed with a crippling condition called collagen disease. Doctors told him that he was unlikely to recover. That's when he put his money where his mouth was. He decided that in addition to the usual treatment, he would add laughter to the mix, literally. I mean it! As part of his treatment, he would seek out things to make him laugh. He believed that would help his recovery, especially since doctors told him he probably wouldn't recover at all.

This was the 1960s, so he didn't have Netflix or a DVD player or even a VCR. Instead, he brought in a movie projector and got hold of his favorite comedy films from the Marx Brothers, and episodes of the TV show *Candid Camera*. He said a couple hours of "genuine belly laughter" would give him pain-free sleep. He called this "laugh therapy," and he went on to write a book about it called *Anatomy of an Illness*—because, for him, laughter turned out to be the best medicine. Sure enough, he got better and lived a long life.

I think Norman Cousins was right on the mark. Laughter can transform your body and your mind for the better. Can it even heal you of a disease? Speaking just for me, yes, I believe it can; I truly do. I say this because I've seen how this has been the experience for so many people in my own life.

This next part is something I don't like to tell a lot because it comes across as self-serving. I don't mean it to be. I'm writing it down here because maybe it will have value for you, and I want to share what's really on my heart. This is something that matters to me greatly because it seems to help people. After a show, people sometimes come up to tell me about how they were sick, and that they want me to know that laughing at my stories and routines and jokes helped them to get better. This happens a lot. Again, I'm not bragging. I'm just telling you that it makes me happy that it happens. I'll just tell one of the stories so you can get an idea of how this goes—and you can read an example of what I am so fortunate to get to hear.

This was a few years ago in Decatur, Alabama, at the Princess Theatre, a beautiful place. After the show, I was at the merchandise table—the "merch" table, they call it—talking with folks and signing things and so forth. A lot of times, it's old home day, you know what I mean? People come to the show year after year and we meet at that merch table every time, and we have a good chat. Anyway, this gentleman and his family came up to me, folks who come out to my show every time I'm in town, every year. They'd even drive to Huntsville and see me there, too.

"But this time," he said, "my dad couldn't come. James, he's had health issues. They've had to amputate his leg."

"They put on a wooden leg, and he's had a hard time dealing with it," he told me. "My daddy doesn't wanna go out in public with it. We tried to get him to come. He's had that leg for six months and he hasn't smiled one time since he had that leg amputated. If I get him on the phone, would you talk to him?"

I said sure. And the next few minutes were a joy of my life.

That man's son got his dad on the phone and said, "Guess who wants to talk to you!" Then he handed that phone over to me. The father knew where his son was going that night so he didn't have to introduce me.

Besides, the way I talk pretty much tells you who it is, even over the phone in Decatur, Alabama.

"Where in the hell are you?" I said, "You should be here! Don't you know I'm doing a show? They tell me that you got a wooden leg. I knew a guy who had a wooden leg. You gotta watch out for a termite problem. Termites get in that leg, you're gonna be back to that hospital again!"

We had this going on the speakerphone and the son started to cry, and he said, "He's laughing! He's laughing!" Pretty soon everybody else started to tear up, me included. Things like that— how do you experience that and not be moved? How can you not believe that smiles and laughter make a difference?

Here's the Story: Everybody Has This One Relative

"I don't know why meatloaf lays on my chest."

I call this the "fat lady" bit. Some people won't like that but I don't mean any offense. Plus that's what I call it everywhere else, so I'm gonna call it that here, too.

When this was a new piece, many years ago, I was doing it at Zanies in Nashville, working out exactly how it should go. This was back when I weighed a whole lot more than I do now and my back had been hurting me for quite a while, so I decided to do the fat lady routine sitting down. It was just two or three lines but still it would give my back a rest. Two nights in a row I did it sitting down—and like a lot of things in comedy, I learned something unexpected just by trying it: When I stood up to continue the show, I found out I couldn't follow the fat lady—it was too funny to follow! So I moved it to the end of the show and made it my closer.

I think the reason it's so popular is because everybody knows somebody like her. She's based on somebody I knew. We'll call her "Aunt Margaret," but that's not her real name and I'm not gonna tell you who it is because her children are still around and they're tougher than me. They could whip my ass.

As I said, the original piece was very brief. It grew over the years. I just kept adding lines as I'd think of them. It eventually got to be eight minutes or more, depending on the night. Just some stuff I just made up and tried out. Other parts of it, I made up while I was on stage. Turns out, a lot of my material comes to me when I'm on stage. And some of it of course really happened. For instance, she really did talk about how everything she ate would "lay on her chest." Also, I remember that Aunt Margaret would get up and walk from the kitchen to the living room couch, which in my parents' house was only a few feet. She would make comments like, "I don't know why my feet hurt like they do." And it was my dad, not me, who said, "I'll take a stab at it."

And that line, "I'm gonna start a diet…starting tomorrow"—that's something I say even today. My neighbor will text me and ask me to go get some dinner, and I'll say, "Sure, I'll start that diet tomorrow."

THOSE SHIRTS

Comedy as a business has changed a lot over the years, but probably never more than in the 1980s, when I was getting started and so many others were, too. The whole industry was being born, you might say. I've heard comedy described as "rock 'n' roll for the 1980s." That's pretty close to it, I think. It was a new version of traditional show business, comedians traveling from town to town every week doing their shows in a comedy club.

As I've said, a lot of comedians were just happy to have a little money in their pocket and to get paid for being funny, but a few comedians were figuring out how to make it a career. A career requires a steady income. One of the ways that income came was when comedians started selling merchandise.

In the early 80s, you'd do your show and that was it. Around 1986, that changed. I was one of the first comedians, maybe the first ever, to sell merchandise. I'd sell it up front after the show, sometimes even before the show. If they had a table, I'd borrow it. If the place didn't have a lobby, I'd go to the sidewalk out front and sell it by the street.

Nobody else was doing that, but I was. Other comedians caught on pretty fast. But as you already know, treating this job like a job, treating show business like a business, has always been important to me. So I was always looking for opportunities to do more business, to make more income, and to better establish myself. In 1991, as the internet became popular, I locked up my website name, funniestman.com. Think back to 1991, if you're old enough to remember it. Nobody had a website, and for sure comedians didn't have websites. A lot of people didn't even know what a website was, and the internet was not at all a part of daily life. But it looked to me like something that was going to be big, so I got in.

It's hard to imagine it now, but it really was the norm that for a long time: the whole comedy business was the live show and nothing else. Except for doing radio and TV interviews, anything beyond your performance hadn't come along yet. Club owners and comedians would make fun of me for selling merchandise, but I had the last laugh. Like I used to say at the end of my show, "My double-wide is paid for."

The first thing I sold was shirts, which I bought from a company in Chattanooga, Tennessee, the same company I would use for the next thirty-plus years. They'd ship those shirts to where I lived in Marietta, Georgia. I'd pick them up at the bus station, then put 'em in the trunk of my car (this will come up again later, by the way), and take them with me to the gig. Later, when I started making enough money to travel a little more comfortably, I'd fly to the city and have the shirt company put them on a Greyhound to that place to save me a step and a little money, too. When I landed, I'd stop by the bus depot to get them. I'd travel with an extra, empty suitcase to take home the few shirts that didn't sell. A lot of other comedians gave me grief about merchandise—right up until they started selling it, too. One time, I remember a comedian had just arrived on the bus for a show. I was at the bus depot to pick up my merchandise. That comedian saw me, and he shouted over to me, "Hey, James Gregory! You still selling trinkets after the show?"

"Yes, I am," I said. "And I use the profits to buy plane tickets!"

You'd think selling shirts would be a simple matter: just order them and sell them at the shows. You certainly could do it that way. A lot of comedians did, and still do. But I'm always thinking about the business aspect, and that's what I was thinking back then. I didn't want what was cheapest or easiest. I wanted what was best for my comedy career, right down to the shirts I sold (and still sell).

I could have saved money by buying inexpensive shirts made of thin cloth, but I didn't do that. I thought about what I'd want myself, if I were buying a shirt for some performer I really liked. If I were going to a comedy show, I wouldn't want just a souvenir shirt that you bought on impulse and then stuck in a drawer. I'd want a shirt I could wear. I'd want something that might be fun to talk about, something I could show other people, something that would last. So that's the kind of shirts I bought, and that's the kind I buy to this day.

Over time, that proved to be a shrewd move, because the folks who have bought my jerseys over the years have worn them for years. To this day, people will show up to my shows wearing a jersey from one of my shows as far back as the 1980s, and that makes me pretty happy, that my customers—my fans—have such good memories of my shows that they'll keep my shirt for twenty-five or thirty years.

It also turned out to be pretty good advertising. Every year, I'd have a different name for my tour, and a lot of people wanted the new shirt every year. There'd be that caricature of me you know on the back, and on the sleeve, it would have the name and the year of the tour. I got what I wanted and so did my fans, so it worked out really well.

Selling merchandise was new for comedians, but other enter-tainers had been doing it for a long time. I got the idea from Hank Williams Jr. I was at my parents' house near Atlanta. Hank Jr. had done two sold-out shows at the Omni. I was reading the Sunday paper and it said he had sold some record number of T shirts, though honestly I don't know who's keeping records of Hank Jr.'s T shirt sales. Anyway, to hear them tell it, he had sold more T shirts at those Atlanta shows than at any other shows in the world. Right then, the thought occurred to me: I oughta do that! I can sell some shirts!

The first bundle of shirts I bought were royal blue with silver lettering. And they didn't come folded. I had to do that. To make it worthwhile, I had ordered a bunch of 'em. You might say I was optimistic. The first time I tried to sell them was at the Comedy Café in Charleston. The week of shows started on Tuesday night and I was out front with my new merchandise, not even in the lobby, just at a table near the door. People would come by at the end of the show and say, *Hey, good show!*—and keep on walking.

I sold a grand total of one shirt—quite a few less than Hank.

I remember somebody at the club telling me, "We're sold out tomorrow! Maybe you'll double your business and sell two shirts!" But I didn't. In fact, the next night, I sold only one again. Now I was up to two. At this point, I was thinking that maybe I had really messed up, buying all these jerseys. Maybe there was a reason Hank Jr. sold shirts and comedians didn't.

The weekend was my last chance. On Friday and Saturday night, there were two shows a night. I had forty-eight shirts left. I sold forty shirts at ten dollars each. That was a pretty good return on my investment. *I got something here,* I thought. As they say, I never looked back. I eventually added a bit about the merchan-dise to remind people it would be there after the show. I've been selling shirts and other merchandise quite successfully ever since. In 1988, I started selling cassettes, which reminds me of another story. I remember being in Las Vegas opening for the great Randy Travis, at that time the biggest star in country music.

Here's how I met Randy. In those days, a man named Bobby Cudd was booking Randy's shows. Bobby is the one who hired me to work for Randy. Bobby is one of those guys that everybody inside the country music business knows and respects. He was and remains one of the top country music agents in Nashville and in the nation. At that time, I was already a headliner in comedy clubs, and it was Bobby who started getting me opportunities beyond the clubs. That show for Randy Travis was quickly followed by another he booked with bluegrass legend Ricky Skaggs. It was a one-nighter in Turlock, California. I flew all the way across the country to do it because it was such a big deal for me personally and professionally. Bobby opened a big door for me. Eventually, he booked me on shows with a whole bunch of country legends, including Tammy Wynette, and many appearances in Las Vegas.

Anyway, on this night in Vegas, I was out in the lobby selling my shirts and cassettes, and I was set up next to Randy's people who were selling his merchandise. A lady came by and asked how much I wanted for a cassette. Tapes at that time were $5.99 and $6.99 in a store. Out there on the table, mine were ten dollars.

"Ten dollars!" she said. "How many songs you have on there?"

"I don't sing," I said.

"Then what's on the tape?"

"I do comedy, ma'am," I said. "I can't sing."

She squared up on me and said, "Did Randy know you couldn't sing before he hired you?"

We all had a good laugh, including Randy's people at his merchandise table next to mine. The next night, I was back in my dressing room when Randy's road manager stuck his head in the door.

"Got a minute?" he said. "Randy wants to talk to you." This didn't sound good. He seemed very serious. A minute later, Randy himself walked in. He pulled over a straight-back chair, turned it around backward, and straddled it to face me. He did not look pleased to be there.

"We might as well get this over with," he said, and then he paused for what seemed like a long, long time. "James," he said, and he looked me in the eye, "how come you didn't tell me before I hired you...that you couldn't sing?" And he nearly fell off the chair laughing.

So merchandise has been very good for me. I still sell merch at shows, but these days we sell a lot more online, including digital downloads and things of that nature. I still talk about it in my shows, but these days I also tell folks where they can see me on social media—including at that website, funniestman.com, I bought over thirty years ago.

LET ME GET YOUR ADDRESS

At first, the reason I had merchandise was to sell it. But pretty quickly I figured out that it's even more valuable when you give it away.

When I go to do a radio show and promote my appearance in a town, I never bring any CDs, DVDs, or shirts into the studio. The trunk of my car may be full of them, but I don't carry any inside with me. If I were to just bring in some and hand them out, I'd be treating my CD like it was a breath mint. "You want one? How about you, ya want one?" That's nothing special.

More importantly, it's also a waste of a valuable opportunity.

Instead. I tell the people who are interviewing me that when I get back to my office, I'll send along a CD or a DVD, "if you'll just give me your address." At this point, you may think that I'm collecting contact information, but that's not it.

When I get back to my office, I do just what I said I'd do, I put a CD in a package and mail it to their address. When it arrives, here's what happens. The radio host says, "Guess what came today? I got a CD in the mail from James Gregory. You remember James Gregory, that funny comedian we had in just last week!" Then they'll spend time on the air talking about me and my show. They might even play part of the CD, or part of the interview we did before. Sometimes they pick up the phone and call while they're on the air.

By treating my CD like something special, I get a whole new round of promotion when I'm not even there. All it costs me is a little time and a piece of merchandise—and they get more good content for their show.

Oh—and I always include a handwritten note. I'll mention that I really appreciated the airtime, because I did, and that I hope to see them again, because I do. Think how you feel when you get a thoughtful, personalized, handwritten note from somebody. When it's in a package with a gift, it's even better. And when someone is following up on what they said they'd do? That's best of all. Think of all the times someone has told you they'd do something but they never followed up. James Gregory follows up. And that gets remembered. In that way, I make my merchandise more valuable by giving it away.

Of course, when I give away things, I'm not always doing it for promotion. Some things you do because it's the right thing to do. I keep an eye on my social media comments. Occasionally I'll hear from someone with family in the hospital with a serious illness, or someone who has lost a loved one. I'll send them a CD or a DVD along with a personal note. On occasion, at the end of a year's tour, we'll send the shirts we have left to a children's hospital, 'cause when you're a kid who's sick, a little surprise like that can lift your spirits. Makes me feel good to do something nice for people. It's what we're all here for, anyway.

***

Radio has always been important for promoting stand-up comedy. Even when social media came along, radio still mattered. Some stations have given up bringing in comedians, and some comedians aren't interested in doing it. But I'm happy to do it. It's my job. I'm working for a living. Besides, if a comedian isn't enthusiastic about appearing on a radio show, that comedian is not going to be very funny on the show, anyway.

I want radio hosts to want me on their show, and I still do radio in every town I visit. Hosts know they'll get a good half hour of entertainment for their listeners—in the business, they say that a strong guest "gives good radio." In the glory days of the comedy club era, I would do five or six live studio shows in every city. There would be in-studio radio on weekday mornings, and on several days, there would be afternoon shows, too. One or two days a week, there would be midday television, and I'd do that, too. If you're in town to do a comedy show, the club is your partner and part of your job is to promote what you're doing there.

A good comedian needs to be ready. He needs to know how to get into his act, meaning he can take a question that has nothing to do with him but still be able to segue into promoting the show. There's more to doing radio and TV promotion than just showing up. Comedians forget that there are more people listening to the radio show than will be at the shows. You can't just say whatever comes to mind. You have to prepare. In every city where I perform, I pick up the local paper and read through it before I go to the studio. That way, if some local reference comes up, I'll know enough to say something funny about it, or at least to use it as a setup to a story I already know. I read about sports, too, even though I am not a sports person. I haven't watched a football game since 1969, when I was trying to impress a girl whose family was crazy about football. But it's my job to be ready to talk about what's going on in the world. At this very minute, I could discuss sports with you better than most people who claim to be fans.

It helps to have a good memory. I've always been good at remembering who I've met and where I've been, plus local references like popular restaurants and stores, and the suburb that everybody make jokes about. (There's always one of those.) And I'm not above making up something for the sake of a joke—or for the sake of a homemade snack. I might say, "Last time I was here, a nice lady brought me some homemade chocolate-chip cookies with pecans in 'em. If that lady is listening right now I have a message for her: cookies don't last forever." It's a funny line, and usually I end up with a plate or two of homemade cookies! (I'm partial to chocolate chip, by the way. In case you just decided to bring me some cookies to the next show.)

One more thing. Whenever I have a morning radio appearance, I wake up at least ninety minutes before I'm supposed to be on the air. I have to have that time to kick the cobwebs out of my head. I need to be awake enough to not look sleepy or sound sleepy, and to be sure I don't yawn. I've actually heard comedians sound sleepy on the radio. How foolish is that? I want every host to know that they are special to me, that I prepared myself for their show, and that their show matters to me. And I want every listener to hear me and say, "You know, this guy is really good. Let's go see him!"

Not every radio appearance is in person. These days, when I'm working in a theater on a weekend, they'll call me a few days before—we call that a "phoner"—and I'll speak to them from my home, or from wherever I happen to be. Same rules apply, though: be up an hour and a half before showtime, prepare for the show, and give them my best effort.

The last thing I'll say is about the last thing I say on the radio. The most important thing is to get people to come to the show. People need to hear the date, the time, and the location.

You probably have heard the old rule from sales, ABC, always be closing. It's the same thing here. The last words out of my mouth will be something like this: "Thanks for having me, fellas. I'll be at Joe's Chuckle House on Friday, Saturday, and Sunday at 7 p.m. Come see me!"

And then I'm off to the next station.

THINKING FOR YOURSELF

Over the years, I've seen a lot of people get into the comedy business, stay a few years, then quit. Most of the time, they blame it on the fact that they're missing birthdays and anniversaries and such. It amazes me that comedians think that way, 'cause they don't have to.

Those are excuses they use because they're not making the progress they'd like. There are a few million people who are making a living who travel, truck drivers and such, and we don't have this scheduling problem. For example, I knew when my parents' fiftieth anniversary was, so I didn't book that week. If you want to be home for your daughter's birthday, don't schedule a show on your daughter's birthday.

You're a lot freer to do that than someone who works nine to five. You have to remember that you're in charge. I don't think a lot of comedians do that. Oh, they think about having their days free, and that they can have a drink at the club when they like, but I'm talking about managing a career. A comedian is self-employed, which means he or she gets to make the decisions. And you have to.

Find me one comedian making $100,000 a year who gave that up for a "regular" job that paid him $40,000 so he could stay home

85

every weekend. If that person's out there, I'll apologize for my opinion, but it'll never happen.

This problem is not unique to comedians. I had an uncle and two cousins who drove eighteen-wheelers. They didn't even have the advantage of being self-employed. They got their schedule from the boss. They'd hit the road for six or seven days, come home for a couple days, go back out a few more days, come back again, around and around like that all year long. Talk about inconvenience! But I'm here to tell you, Uncle Charlie and Aunt Ruby raised seven kids doing that. You make your choices to get the things you want. Turns out that not everybody thinks very hard about what they really want, though, and what it might cost in time and effort.

Most reasons for getting out of comedy are excuses. It's not "too demanding." It's not "too hard." These comedians just failed to plan the life they claim they want, and refused to recognize that the job is more than what you do on stage.

I remember making a four-hundred-mile drive home with a comedian friend after a February gig in Raleigh, North Carolina. He'd been opening for me that week. He said, "I really need to be working next week but I'm taking some time off. I haven't had a week off since New Year's Eve."

It was February and he hadn't had a week off since…New Years? That was six weeks before! Most Americans get a week or two off once a year.

I've worked more hours and worked harder at this job than at any of the many, many jobs I've ever had. Schedule your work around your life, but remember that it's still a job, and you have to show up for it. This is where the comedian's mindset of "I work a half hour a day!" gets you: it's not just the time on stage. When you start treating it like a job that requires no more than a half hour a day, pretty soon you start to believe it. That's the beginning of the end. That's when the audiences start to get bored with you. That's when the club owners stop booking you.

***

When you get into the entertainment business when you're thirty-six, the way I did, and if you've been working at something else, you've already developed a work ethic. Before I got into comedy, I had been a salesman, and that meant I was doing work I had to think about and do well. The experience gave me an excellent foundation for what I would do as a professional comedian. In particular, I understood business, which is what so many people in entertainment never figure out. In that way I was fortunate.

I was planning some dates in Nashville. It was 1987 and the comedy scene was blowing up everywhere, but Nashville was especially big. It had long had only one comedy club, the world-famous Zanies, one of the oldest comedy clubs outside of New York and LA. But in a very short time, Nashville went from having one comedy venue to seven. This meant I had a decision to make—not a decision based on what I liked or didn't like. I had to make a business decision.

Lenny Sisselman is my personal manager, but at the time he was the manager of Zanies in Nashville. I had worked his club since I first went on the road. I did well for his club and he did right by me. We had a history. But now there were other rooms in the city, and I had to make a choice. Zanies was and remains the best room in town, really one of the nicest rooms in the country. I could have based my decision on that fact alone, but that's not the wise way to do business. I had to look at this as a businessman.

In those days, the pay structure was simple. You'd do a certain number of shows and the club would pay you a set amount. For most comedians, that was a pretty good deal. You didn't have to be famous. You didn't have to be out there promoting yourself all that much. All you had to do was show up, do your act, and pick up your check. You got paid no matter how many people showed up or how many drinks got sold. (Though if nobody comes out to see you, you'll sure have a problem getting booked next time.) But if you had a bit of a following, there was a way to make more. The big-name, national comedians had figured it out. Some of us working the road were starting to figure it out, too.

I went to Lenny and told him I wanted what's called a *door deal*. Instead of paying me a set amount, we'd split the ticket sales, a certain percentage for each of us. I wasn't very famous, but I was becoming what's known as a *draw*, meaning people really would come out to see me because it was me, not just because they wanted whatever comedian was in town. With a door deal, we'd be in business together. We'd both have a reason to promote the show and bring in the biggest audience we can. (See how those comedians treating it like "I only work a half hour a day!" end up having to quit the business?)

So this door deal was on the table with Lenny in a town with half a dozen clubs. I found out later that nobody had ever offered him that kind of deal. He was used to writing a check to the talent and being done with it. But I'd been doing these door deals other places, and doing well. That included the clubs in other cities owned by these new guys in Nashville.

Lenny told me he could give me a raise, but that he couldn't offer me the deal I wanted where we share the profit and the risk. So I made up my mind. We parted ways. There were no hard feelings, either. It was strictly business, not personal. For the next couple years, when I came to town, I worked for his competitors. As the comedy boom faded, so did those other venues. I was managing my career carefully, but perhaps those other rooms couldn't keep up with the times. Lenny could and did, though, and eventually I was back at Zanies. I've been there ever since.

Since I'm talking about the money side of comedy here, I want you to know that nobody made a big mistake here, not Lenny for passing on me and not me for going across town. I was getting popular but I wasn't in any way as well-known as I would be years later. If he had done the door deal, he might have made less money than in the traditional paycheck arrangement. A door deal was and is about sharing risk. Plus, the whole comedy business was coming through growing pains, as they say. We were all figuring things out, and that was a good thing.

By the way, those other clubs in Nashville were competing with each other, but that was a good thing, too. In fact, as the boom grew, the local TV stations would have Lenny on to talk about comedy—he was the local expert, after all, running the only club the city had had for most of a decade. He'd never bash the other clubs. They'd ask what he hoped would happen, and he'd say, "I hope they do it right." He had figured out something that all of us were figuring out: a rising tide lifts all boats. If the audience liked comedy at one club, they'd probably start going to the others. And if one of those new clubs put on a lousy show, that might be the first comedy show somebody had ever seen, and it would be their last. We were all in it together.

Not every town was as friendly with competitors as that. The thing is that it's smart to be friendly that way. If you go to a town where there's a thriving comedy scene, a lot of up-and-coming performers, and a lot of good stages, you can be sure there's a friendly relationship among pretty much everybody. That's because they understand that this is a tight-knit industry where quality needs to be high—and needs to be encouraged—all around. That's good for comedians, good for the audience, and good for the comedy business. Always will be.

***

I respect club owners, probably because they think about business as much as I do. We see things the same way, by and large. I admire them. I do not badmouth them. Of course, some comedians will badmouth club owners. I think that's very foolish, because none of us today would be around if not for those club owners. These are people who took the risk of opening a comedy club where we could make a living, having no certainty that the business was going to work out. Some of these guys could have lost everything, yet they went ahead and built the stage we're all tap-dancing on today. Without those club owners around the country, I wouldn't be in this business.

The usual comedy show today goes like it did back in the '80s: the emcee does fifteen minutes, the feature does twenty-five minutes, and the headliner closes with forty-five. Figure another five minutes for announcements and for performers coming on and off stage, and that makes a ninety-minute show. In the '80s, most of the people in the audience were coming to a comedy show for the first time. It was the job of the emcee to hit the stage with energy and get people comfortable. There were always a few things you had to do, encourage people to check out the drink specials and maybe order something to eat, remind them who's on the show and who's coming next week, get the audience ready for a good time. After doing all that first, the emcee could do his own jokes.

One night, at the very start of my career, when I was working as an emcee in Atlanta, I went to the club manager, Chris DiPetta. "I can't get any traction," I said. "Could I hit the stage and do my act right away, then make all those announcements at the end?" He said he would ask Ron DiNunzio, whom I've mentioned before, one of the founders of the club. The next night I walked in and Ron was waiting for me. While I have great respect for my old friend, Ron, I'm not telling tales out of school when I tell you he didn't have a great sense of humor about these things.

"Chris says you've become a big star now," he said. "Says you don't want to make announcements."

"Ron, I didn't say that," I said.

"I know what you said," he told me, even though that wasn't what I'd said at all. He didn't like my idea, but before I could say anything, he gave me his answer. "All right," he said. "Let's try it." He could have said no. But in the end, he said, *Yeah, go ahead.* And I did, which was a big boost for me. And it worked out just fine.

Years later, Ron and I figured out something else that was valuable—maybe even more valuable in dollars and cents. At this time, Ron and Dave had moved their business office out of the club and into the complex across the parking lot. My office was down the sidewalk from that. One day, I was in their office booking my upcoming dates when Ron mentioned that I had sold out all nine of my shows that week, and that six of those were over the weekend.

"When the audience goes into work on Monday, they're talking about how much fun they had seeing this comedian, and their friends will want to go see him," Ron said. "But that comedian? He's already gone."

And that would have been the end of the conversation, just a thought, just a passing fact we all knew about the comedy business, but it gave me an idea. "Why don't we try doing two weeks?" I said.

"In a row?" Ron said. "Nobody does two weeks."

"Let's try it," I said, and I meant it. I thought we might be onto something. He called his partner Dave, who had the same reaction: it just wasn't how anybody does things in the comedy business. In those days, a comedian worked a week and moved on. Nobody did two weeks in a row, not ever. You might come back in a year—six months, if you were a draw—but two weeks in a row? That was unheard of.

"I know, but let's try it anyway," I said. They knocked it around a bit and eventually agreed. To protect themselves, they insisted we do it in the "worst" month, meaning some time when crowds were down. For them, that was June. Ron even told me why he thought it wasn't going to work. "That's when it's still broad daylight at 9 p.m., plus people are going on vacations, or going to graduations, or getting married," he said.

"Yeah, sure," I said. "I'll take it."

After we added up the receipts, we found out just how well it had worked: very, very well. Of course, it was clear early on from the big crowds. We both made money, and that changed things not just for me and for Ron, but for other comedians and club owners, too. I had come up with something new and it made more money for all of us.

It went so well that once other places found out that it worked in Atlanta, they started doing it in their own rooms. And the industry changed and grew again. This comedy industry had come out of nothing. It had grown up far from New York and LA.

We made it anyway. We had the right people and the right attitude—comedians and club owners who understood that show business really is business, and that you can make it work if you work hard.

Here's the Story: Lawn Mower Repair and Income Tax Service

"You did a helluva job on this mower. I think I'll let you do my taxes."

When I was living with my parents as I started doing comedy, I would walk a lot, and that's when I started noticing signs. This was a real sign. I believe the place I saw it was on Ponce deLeon Avenue in Decatur, Georgia, back in the 1980s.

I've found other signs, of course, but I couldn't always make 'em work as a joke. One time I saw one that said, "Daycare Center and Landfill." It was out in front of a small ranch house with a bunch of dump trucks next to it and a garage in back—and, I guess, a landfill behind all that. I had a joke about how I thought they were filling up the landfill, but I could never quite make it work. It was funny to me, though.

GETTING ALONG WITH EACH OTHER

When my father passed away in January 1995, it changed me. Whenever you lose a parent, it's going to affect you, but when you're a comedian, it's likely that people will see some of that change. When my dad passed, I started to tell more stories on stage, not about my father, necessarily, but about life and family. I became more introspective, maybe more socially relevant, you might say.

I was pissed off for a while, too. I moved a little away from being strictly a teller of jokes to someone who had something more to say. I had also reached a point where I knew how to do that, how to say more things that mattered to me and still bring the audience along—because what I do, first and foremost, is comedy. I am an entertainer, not a preacher, not a politician. So if I have something to say, it still has to be funny when I say it.

I don't do comedy about politics, but how I feel about things comes out. I believe with all my heart that we have to treat each other with kindness. There can't be room in your heart for bigotry. Awful bigotry has happened in the world, of course, but that's no excuse for flipping the old prejudice into some new prejudice and calling that the right thing to do. It's not right, not at all.

Being a Southern man, I feel strongly about this. A lot of people who never lived in the South act like they know everything about it. They'll even try to tell you about how it was before they were born. Truth is, they don't know. They weren't there. I was. You can find bigots anywhere you go, but that does not mean a whole place is bad. Where I grew up in the South, there were bigots, but that's true everywhere you go, north or South. In those days, and it's still this way, neighbors would help neighbors, and they didn't worry about the color of your skin. That's the life I grew up in.

I think we can solve a lot of our problems if we focus on treating each other as individuals. I choose my friends based on who they are, not on race and not on politics. If someone is different politically from me, so what? But in today's society, there's a lot of people that want you to pick your friends—and especially your enemies—based on politics. Building up barriers between human beings, shutting down communication, is not the way to change hearts and minds.

People get past their problems by embracing love, not hate. Martin Luther King Jr. was one of the all-time greatest heroes in this country. When he crossed that bridge in 1965 in Selma, he and the people marching with him knew they were going to get cracked in the head. They went ahead anyway because it was the right thing to do. They believed in what Dr. King believed, that people should "not be judged by the color of their skin but by the content of their character." Makes all the sense in the world. Why should people think you're anything special—or anything bad—because of the color of your skin? The Civil Rights Act of 1964 was a good thing. It should have come earlier. It made life better for a lot of people and it pointed us in the right direction.

If we aim to treat each other better and fail to do it perfectly, that doesn't make us hypocrites. That makes us human. So I won't criticize anybody for trying to be something better and failing to reach it. We are in this together, as they say. Treat others equally and fairly. Do unto others as you would have them do unto you— that's what I learned in Sunday school, but you don't have to have gone to church to choose to know it or to act on it. It'll take you a long way.

***

You hear people say all the time they want to change the world, but that's not how it works.

The world is nothing but people, and people change one at a time, one heart at a time, one mind at a time. Here's the toughest truth of all, the truth people don't want to accept: for change to be permanent, you have to change yourself. Oh, we can encourage people and help out, but real change comes when an individual says *I used to live and believe this way, but now I'm going to live and believe another way*. We can—and we should—encourage people to get along regardless of the color of their skin, but only they can change their own hearts.

Most people alive today are too young to have lived through segregation, but when I went to school it was the law of the land. I've seen it up close, and I'm here to tell you that racism and hate are not only evil, they are dumb. The people who do it look stupid, and it's always been like that.

My daddy felt was the same way. When I was a kid, I'd go out every morning and wait by the road for the bus to take us to Lithonia Elementary School. The bus would come by and stop at every white person's house. A kid would get on the bus, and that bus would take him to the segregated school, the school that was for whites only, the place we called the "white school." A few minutes later another bus would come by, except that one stopped where the black families lived. It took those kids to a different school.

At that time of the morning, my dad had usually gone to work already, but I remember one day he was still at home and he saw this. "That's stupid as shit," he said. "Those kids know each other. They play games together, they run together, they get in trouble together. They oughta just pick 'em up together and let 'em go to whatever school they want."

That was my daddy talking, and he was right. It took a few more years before the government caught up with my daddy's way of thinking.

GOOD GUYS

In the '80s and '90s, when we worked on the road, club owners didn't put you up in a hotel. They put you up in an apartment that they'd leased. Comedians called it the "comedy condo."

I hated those places.

Most of them weren't very nice, there was little privacy, they could get noisy, and you had constant company with the other comedians, whether you liked them or not. It's hard enough living with a roommate. Try living with a new one every week, two if the opener wasn't local.

Yet looking back, those years were the best thing that ever happened to me. Being around those comedians who had a lot of experience, I saw how easy it was to settle into a routine that led nowhere—exactly what I did not want to do. I saw so many comedians party away their paycheck week after week, and never become a bigger draw or improve what they were doing. Their examples were big motivators for me. Seeing that made me start treating comedy like a real job.

The condo years brought me into contact with good examples, too. I met some people who were very talented, very interesting, and who had great work habits and a great work ethic that I could learn from. So, while a lot of comedians showed me what not to do, a few taught me what I needed to start doing. They made me better.

One of the guys I learned from was Steven Wright. We were sharing the condo at a club in Oklahoma. Steven had made a huge splash on *The Tonight Show* in 1982. I was hanging out with him about eighteen months later, in 1984. I think Johnny Carson knew from the start that Steven was going to be big. He was grinning when he introduced him. "I think you're going to find him … a little different," he said. Steven's now-famous deadpan delivery was such a smash that the Carson show brought him back less than a week later, which had never happened before to a comedian. He deserved it because he was, and is, that good. He's also very smart about how he works. Here's what I learned from him.

As popular as he was, Steven could have stayed anywhere, but he wanted to stay in the condo. I lived in a condo every week. I would usually wake up earlier than the guys I was sharing the space with, mostly because a lot of those guys stayed up late every night and slept most of the day. The week I was with Steven, I got up at my usual time, but in this case, I wasn't the first one up. There was Steven sitting on the floor cross-legged with a cassette player on one knee and a pen and legal pad on the other. He'd hit play, listen closely, then hit stop and write something down, then he'd rewind it and do it again. Steven recorded every show he did. The next morning he'd go over it, study how he performed and how the audience had reacted, write down what he'd done, and look for ways to improve. I had never seen anybody do that, but if it was good enough for Steven, I figured it was a good idea for me, so I started doing it, too.

One of the first things I learned from that, and I learned it immediately, was to slow down. I don't mean "slow down" the way Jim McCawley meant it at *The Tonight Show*. I mean that I learned to wait a bit after the punchline before I started the next bit or routine. As soon as I started recording my shows, it became clear to me that I was talking over the laughter. I would be going into my next routine while they were still laughing at the last one. That's called "stepping on the laugh," and you don't want to do that. Obviously, the idea is to get as many laughs, and as big laughs as you can, from each routine. That's good for the performer and good for the audience. It makes a far more enjoyable show, and it's an improvement that comes just from delivery, what you might call the technical side, not from writing another joke. It adds a lot of value, a lot of "punch" to any comedian's material. I have mentioned several times here that my ability to "say things funny" is a big part of why I've been successful. One of the things that separates a good comedian from a very successful comedian is just that, being able to make good material into great material by delivery. This kind of thing is part of that.

If not for watching Steven review his recorded show every day, it would not have occurred to me to record my show and get better that way. It's amazing how the show sounds different afterward than when you're up there doing it. When you're in your bedroom by yourself, listening to your show, you have those moments you need where you go, "Damn, that's not so good." In my opinion, you have to record your show and study it if you want to make it to the top rank of comedians. Over the years, the best ones have always done it, folks like Robert Klein (I was told he was the first to record his shows), Jerry Seinfeld, Larry Miller, and the great Steven Wright.

If you've seen Steven perform, you might find it interesting to know that that voice of his is the same onstage and off. It's just one of the things that makes him such a fun, funny guy to hang out with. During that week, he and I had lunch together every day.

We went to the same place, the Village Inn Pancake House across the interstate. I remember heading over there one day and he said, "We could walk across the highway."

I said, "Steven, come on. It's an interstate. I'll get the car. We'll go down the access road to the next exit and drive across."

"Nah. Let's just walk across."

"Steve, I'm not gonna walk across the interstate. If you really wanna walk, I'll walk with you down the access road and around, but I'm not walking across the interstate."

I eventually talked him out of walking through traffic, but he didn't let go of it easy. I'll never forget how he said it in that dead-pan voice of his. "It would be a challenge, a real challenge," he said.

Another night during that week, Jay Leno was in town to do a theater show. After he finished, he came to the comedy club to see Steven do the late show. This was long before Jay was the host of *The Tonight Show*, so you may not know that he was already a big star in the comedy world. For all intents and purposes, he was a regular on the Letterman show. Every month or so, he'd do a spot on Friday night where he'd sit at the desk with Dave and do material. Dave would often begin by asking Jay, "What's your beef?"

"What's my beef? What's my beef?" Jay would say with a grin and a sneer, then he'd launch into all kinds of fantastic material. It was these unforgettable Friday night appearances that first made him famous beyond the clubs and made him popular with comedians and fans alike. It is probably why he was promoted to host *The Tonight Show* instead of Letterman after Carson retired. I tell you all this because, once upon a time, Jay Leno wasn't just the friendly host of a late-night show. He was one of the most admired stand-up comedians ever, and that's the truth.

This night with Steven Wright wasn't the first time I'd been around Jay. We had worked together the year before, in Atlanta in

1983. Paul Clay was a local comedian and he opened the show, I was the feature, and Jay was the headliner. After those shows, we'd go over to the Beef Cellar, a popular place among entertainers because they served meals until early in the morning. I remember sitting there with Jay and Paul. We were stuffing ourselves and Jay was giving us advice—useful stuff, the kind of advice a comedian couldn't get anywhere else or from anyone else. (I remember the Beef Cellar for another reason, too. It wasn't just a late-night place; it was also a hangout for comedians just getting started, which meant we didn't always have much money. Sometimes the owner would take pity on us and let us go without a check—he'd ask us to take care of the waitress and that would be enough. Life is full of decent people that you never forget.)

Anyway, it was *that* Jay Leno, before he was a household name, that came across town to say hi to Steven and to support him. When we came off stage, Jay and Steve wanted to get something to eat. After a late-night show, it's not easy in most towns to find a place still open, but that wasn't a problem here. There was a place called Pete Mesquite's, a steak joint just across the parking lot. (As the emcee that week, I would announce at every show that if you took your ticket stub to Pete Mesquite's you could get 20 percent off your dinner. It's funny what you remember.)

Jay was there to see Steven and he asked me to come along anyway, and of course I went. These were two of the biggest comedians in America! So we sat down to eat, and even though it was very late, people were still out and of course they recognized Jay. Almost as many recognized Steven. Every few minutes, somebody would come over to the table and they'd start with an apology. "I hate to interrupt your dinner..." and then they'd ask for an autograph. (This was before cellphones, so nobody was getting a picture because nobody was walking around with a camera.) Just like he is today, Jay was a class act. He would sign everything they put in front of him and greet every person who came by to say hello. Then the person would notice Steven Wright and they'd get him to sign, too. This happened several times over the course of a couple hours, but every time, when the person would turn to go, Jay would call them back.

"Hey, wait a minute. You wanna get this guy's autograph, too," he'd say, and he'd point to me. "This is James Gregory. He might be famous someday. You better get his autograph while you can." He might not have believed I was going to be famous, but he wanted that fan to show respect. It was total kindness. Jay's a real class act.

A SOUTHERN ACCENT BUT NOT A SOUTHERN COMEDIAN

People think of me as a Southern comedian, but the truth is that I'm a comedian for everybody.

For instance, I've made a lot of trips to Portland, Oregon, and I've worked Seattle, San Jose, made a lot of trips to St. Louis, and done many shows in Chicago. In fact, I've worked in thirty-three of the fifty states, and the only reason I haven't hit the others is that there are only fifty-two weeks in a year. When the Punchline gave me the opportunity to do two weeks in a row in June and December, I started doing that more often, and from that, the dominoes started to fall—in a good way. Once the club in Raleigh found out I would do two weeks back-to-back, they wanted me to do it for them, too. Other clubs followed suit and I was pleased to take the work because it meant less travel and more money. Pretty soon, I had eight cities booking me for two-week runs twice a year, including Atlanta; Columbia, South Carolina; Augusta, Georgia; Raleigh, North Carolina; and Birmingham, Alabama.

By the mid-1990s, that meant I was booking thirty-two weeks in only eight cities, all door deals, and they all happened to be in the southeastern United States. Comedy is a business, and this was and remains a very good way to do business. I could still work in, say, Seattle, but why would I? Let me be frank with you. In Seattle, I could book only a week at a time, I'd get paid a salary instead of a portion of the ticket sales, and I'd have to travel across the country and back, all to make maybe a quarter of what I would make for a show in the Southeast. I was making great money with less travel and less effort.

Then I started adding what a lot of people call one-nighters but I call weekenders, because that's what they are. Another old friend, Brad Greenberg, owned the Comedy Zone chain of clubs. He booked these weekenders in places like Greensboro and Macon, smaller cities that might not be able to support a week of shows but could for sure get audiences for five shows across a Friday and Saturday. Add his five cities to the work I already had, and that meant I had more than forty weeks a year booked before I could even consider where else I might go. So that's why it narrowed down. It's not like I planned to stay in the Southeast. It was all just arithmetic to me.

You may be wondering though if the audiences were receptive in those places outside the South. That's one of those questions journalists ask in almost every interview, so I've known this answer for many years because I've had to give it for so long. I used to resent being asked this, but I don't resent it anymore. I suppose time makes you a little less worked up about things. Anyway, it used to annoy me for people to refer to me as a Southern comedian. If you've seen me perform in person, or watched a clip of me on YouTube, you realize that there's nothing in my act where I talk about the South. I don't talk about it. I don't use the word *Southerner*. When I do my show in, say, Massachusetts, I don't change a word. It's the same story I tell in Birmingham, Alabama, which is about as far south on the map as you can get.

One time a reporter asked me about all this and I said, "Have you ever referred to Jerry Seinfeld as a Northern comedian? Guys from that part of the country toured the South long before they became famous. If you go to Zanies in Nashville or the Punchline in Atlanta, their pictures are still there on the wall from when they came through in the early days. Do you ask them if they are Northern comedians?" Of course, the answer is not ever, not even one time. But somehow, it works if it's the other way. To them, I'm a Southern comedian.

Audiences like me outside the South not because I'm Southern, but because I make people laugh no matter where they're from. For example, this happened while I was touring with Randy Travis as his opening act. We did a show in Hyannis Port, Massachusetts, and on this evening, I did something very unusual: I added a local reference—a very local reference. At that time, I would start my show by mentioning how far away the place was from where I live in Georgia, then I'd tell them about driving there and go into my usual routine about my fear of flying. This time, I added a little local color. "I'm afraid to fly. To make sure I get here safely, I drive. Well," I said, and I paused for a moment, "I drive... unless I'm with Ted Kennedy." Believe it or not, I rocked the room. They exploded with laughter—in Kennedy country! A few of them stood up.

So how did I get to be known by a lot of folks as a Southern comedian? I have a Southern accent. That's it. That's the whole thing.

And that accent comes in handy these days. Comedians build a following on social media. I have a big social media presence that I'm proud of. On some of those platforms, I have more subscribers than most of the other so-called Southern comedians. But before that stuff came along, I had to build my following in other ways, and I started out building an audience by getting on the radio.

As I've said, network television wasn't all that interested in me, probably because they don't understand what I'm telling you here: I sound Southern, but what I talk about connects with everybody, no matter where they're from. For a lot of TV producers, that's hard for them to believe, because they think about demographics more than they think about whether or not something is just flat-out funny. The TV I did do gave me pockets of support, and those fans have always been enthusiastic—I'm thinking of the Nashville Network, where I appeared several times on *Nashville Now* with Ralph Emery.

But radio was very good to me, and I think the people I'll mention here would agree that I was good for their shows, too. Through all these years, I have made thousands of appearances on shows that are broadcast coast-to-coast on hundreds of stations. Besides all the local stations, there were syndicated shows where I had a blast every time: John Boy and Billy out of Charlotte, Rick and Bubba out of Birmingham, Bob and Tom broadcasting from Indianapolis, and Steve and DC from St. Louis. My voice is recognizable—I don't think that's in dispute, do you? People started keeping up with me because I was funny and they liked me as a character on stage, but there was one more thing: my voice just stuck in their heads!

When I was in Bahrain doing shows for the troops, I was having breakfast one morning in a nice hotel. This was a very international setting, very upscale, a businessman's hotel, and people of all kinds were walking by, some in the usual suit and tie, some with kufis or hijabs on their heads and wearing traditional Muslim clothing. (I had to look this one up: a kufi is a short, round cap that a lot of Islamic men wear. A hijab is that scarf a lot of Islamic women wear. Fine with me. Wear whatever you want!)

I was sitting there talking with my manager—I was still recovering from that scary flight—when all of a sudden somebody came over to me, put his hand on my shoulder, and said, "I'd recognize that voice anywhere." We were in Bahrain! But it's the same thing that has happened to me for years across the United States in restaurants, cafés, coffee shops, truck stops, you name it. I'm a regular at the Waffle House. Every time—I mean every time—I'm in a Waffle House, somebody in the booth behind calls me out, and they always say the same thing: *I know that voice!*

This voice I've got? You might say it put me on the map, from the Waffle House to the Middle East.

Here's the Story: Ribs at the Petro Truck Stop

"It's a truck stop, a truck stop, a truck stop… there's three acres of eighteen wheelers out front, it's a truck stop! There's real men in there. We go in, we sit down, two comedians, surrounded by truckers…."

This is one of those stories where something happened in real life, then I changed it around and added a whole lot of pieces to make it funnier. Like the part about asking for raspberry vinaigrette dressing and having a waitress with no teeth and mustard on her apron. "Old mustard," I'd say. "It was crunchy." About the only part that really happened the way I said was that we were in a truck stop having a bite to eat. The fellow who inspired the story is one of my favorite people, a very funny comedian from Nashville named Keith Alberstadt. He would go on to appear on the late-night shows with Letterman, Seth Meyers, and Stephen Colbert, but this happened before all that, the first time he went out on the road with me.

One afternoon, we went to get a bite to eat at a Petro truck stop somewhere in North Carolina. They had a restaurant called the Iron Skillet, and it had a buffet with barbecued ribs. Keith got himself some of those good ribs, but instead of eating them with his fingers, he was taking them on with a knife and fork, cutting the meat off the bones. It made perfect sense: he didn't want to mess up his hands. But I thought it was hilarious. About that time, Lenny called to ask me how things were going. I told him I couldn't work with Keith anymore. "He's eating ribs in a truck stop with a knife and fork!" We had a good laugh over it, and that became the basis of that whole piece about "a young guy" in a truck stop.

As you know, I came up with a lot more to build it out, like asking if the lettuce in the salad had been treated with any kind of pesticides. I had the waitress say, "We spray for roaches every now and then. I don't think any of 'em got into the lettuce."

MY FRIENDS IN COUNTRY MUSIC

There's something about the country music industry that's a little bit different from other parts of show business. I find that the people in the country music business are more down to earth. I've been fortunate to meet a lot of them.

Probably the biggest name in country music, one of the biggest in music, period, was George Jones. I got to become good friends with George and his wife, Nancy. George even gave me a nickname. In 1998 I had an album and a tour called "Grease, Gravy & John Wayne's Momma." From then on, George called me "The Gravy Man." When I worked the club in Nashville, he and his wife would come to see my show, and a number of times we went out to dinner. George would never talk about country music, though. Like a true gentleman, he always turned the conversation away from himself and to his guest. He'd ask me where I'd traveled lately and where I was headed next, things like that. Mostly, though, he wanted to talk about comedy. One night, we were at dinner along with Keith Bilbrey (more about him in a minute) and his wife, Emy Joe. George was talking about comedy and finally, he said, "I wish I could be funny!"

His wife wasn't gonna let that pass. "Oh, God help me!" she said. George loved a good laugh and he was such a nice guy—like I said, a real down-to-earth fellow I was fortunate to be friends with. When he passed away, they had a viewing before the funeral and they invited a few people to join the family. Keith Bilbrey reached out to me to say that he thought Nancy would want me there, so of course I came over. As she and I stood at the casket, she put her arm around me and just wouldn't turn loose. "You will never know how much you made George laugh," she said, and she squeezed me so tight. My friendship with George and Nancy has meant a great deal to me, and I feel privileged for it. I'm glad for the good times we all had. I'm glad I could make George laugh!

By the way, you know Keith Bilbrey even if you never heard the name. He is the most famous announcer in the history of country music, including nearly thirty years as the voice of the Grand Ole Opry. In country music, Keith knows everybody, and everybody knows Keith. One time he was doing his afternoon radio show on Nashville's WSM. I was in town and Keith had just been to the show. He proceeded to give me the kind of promotion you just can't buy. "James Gregory's in town this week and you don't want to miss this show," he said. "I didn't miss it! And let me tell you who else did not miss it last night." He then listed everyone who'd been there, crowded into a cramped greenroom. It was a who's who of country music: George and Nancy Jones, Brad Paisley, Kenny Chesney, "Whispering Bill" Anderson, Jan Howard, and more. They all loved comedy, we were all friends, and it was kind of an "old home day" to see them. And for Keith to promote the show like he did on the biggest country radio station in the world? That was just awesome.

Thinking about Keith Bilbrey makes me think of another friend, Ray Stevens. He is a legend—a comedian, performer, and songwriter, and not just of funny songs, though Lord knows he's written hundreds of funny songs like "The Streak" and so many others. He also wrote "Misty," which was already a classic when Ray recorded a bluegrass version himself and made it a hit all over again.

Anyway, Keith makes me think of Ray because when Ray was inducted into the Country Music Hall of Fame in 2019, Keith and I performed "The Streak." We were a surprise to Ray—he didn't know we were going to be there. The Hall of Fame people had reached out to numerous people to surprise Ray. I was the eyewitness—maybe you remember it from the record. The action news reporter was Keith, naturally, since he was already famous for talking on the radio. He knew all the lines. I may have said my line different because I didn't know we were supposed to memorize the script. But between a little quick thinking and the teleprompter, we did just fine and got Ray into the Hall of Fame, where he belongs.

By the way, one of the few times I did some acting, it was Ray that put me up to it. In 1995 he made a funny movie called *Get Serious*. He cast me as the no-good lawyer out to get him. My character's name was Harold P. Cheatham, from the law firm of Robb, Cheatham, and Steele. (Say it out loud.) As I say, I'm not an actor, and on that day, I proved it. I had done two takes when the director took me aside and said, "James, you're trying to be an actor. Don't be an actor. Be a goofy lawyer." Acting goofy is something I can do, so that's just what I did. On the very next take, I got it, and that's the one you'll see if you look it up on YouTube.

You might wonder how I met all these people. Some I met at my shows, but I also met a lot doing a TV show called *Nashville Now*, the nightly talk show hosted for years by Ralph Emery on The Nashville Network. They say that James Brown was the "hardest working man in show business," but anybody who said that never met Ralph Emery. He was live on Nashville television every morning before sunrise—he came on before *The Today Show*—then he'd wrap that up and go host a radio show in the middle of the day, and a national television show at night.

Over the years, I made numerous appearances on *Nashville Now*. I'm here to tell you it was a little different from *The Tonight Show* and *Letterman*. Those shows were taped in advance, but Ralph went on live. That made it a little more spontaneous, a little looser—also a little more dangerous. Plus, unlike the planning and staff writing that goes into those other shows, *Nashville Now* really was Ralph's show. Between that and going out live, it actually made me a little nervous.

On every talk show I've ever done, they want you to come on and do your new material, give the audience something they haven't seen on the show before. Not Ralph. He never hesitated to ask me to do some favorite routine. Didn't matter if I'd done it on the show already. If that's what he wanted to hear, he'd ask. "Are you going to do that one tonight?" he'd say.

"I hadn't planned on it, Ralph, but I will if you want," I'd tell him.

Another way it was different was that it really was Ralph's show, and being live meant he had the last word. I'd give the producer a card that had what Ralph oughta ask me that night, but there was no guarantee Ralph would ask those questions. That would occasionally lead to an awkward moment. One night, I was doing a routine he'd asked for about a fat lady. Afterward, we were talking at the desk and he said, "So, how much do *you* weigh?"

Folks, this went out on live TV! I couldn't say what I wanted to say, which was, *What the hell, Ralph?* But I sure wanted to.

Another night at the desk, I got what I believe was the biggest laugh in the ten-year run of the show. We were talking about the movie *Amadeus*, since it had just won the Oscar for Best Picture.

"James, have you ever thought about being an actor?" Ralph said.

"Not really," I said.

"But do you think you'd like to be in a movie?" he said.

"Well, I guess I could be in a movie," I said. I was trying to ad lib, to steer us toward something funny in the conversation, so I said, "Maybe I could, Ralph. As long as I got to keep my clothes on." That got a mild laugh.

"Would you be in a movie nude for a million dollars?" Ralph said.

I didn't miss a beat. "For a million dollars, I'd sleep with the Hager Twins." The place blew up. Ralph couldn't calm us down—not me, not the audience, not even himself. He finally had to give up and go to commercial.

In case you don't know, the Hagers were identical twin brothers who played and sang together starting in the 1960s. They went on to be cast members on *Hee Haw* for seventeen years. They were also young and handsome and had appeared in *Playgirl* holding a banjo and a guitar, strategically placed. They were well-known and well-liked in Nashville. If you lived there in those days, you had probably run into them around town.

While we tried to compose ourselves during the commercial break, Ralph's stage manager came over. Actually, he was more than the stage manager. He was Ralph's right-hand man in broadcasting. Everybody called him Killer, and anybody who'd done a TV or radio appearance with Ralph knew him—so of course Killer knew everybody in country music.

Killer leaned down to me and whispered, "I just got off the phone. The Hager Twins are on their way."

I said the first thing that came to mind. "Do they have a million dollars?"

We all busted out laughing again. We tried to get it together before the commercial break was over, but I'm not sure we did.

They broadcast *Nashville Now* from a studio in the Opryland complex northeast of the city. You could walk directly outside from the *Nashville Now* greenroom. There were a couple double-wide trailers out there, one for private dressing rooms and the other as a production office. Behind that, though, was a lovely home where one man lived by himself. He had moved there after his wife passed away, and now he lived just a few steps from the Opry itself, where he performed every week. He'd even greet guests to the Opryland theme park, and sometimes he'd show up early for the Opry to help the staff with odd jobs like stocking sodas in the refrigerators backstage—like I said, country music people are different in a good way.

The man who lived in that house was Roy Acuff, "The King of Country Music."

When the weather was good, they'd set up a few picnic tables for us just outside the greenroom. You could duck out for a few minutes for a bite to eat, to take a smoke break, and to visit with the crew and the other guests. This is where I first met the famous Mr. Roy Acuff. There were five or six of us shooting the bull, waiting for the show to start, when Mr. Roy, as he was known, walked up and sat down with us. He didn't know me so to start a conversation, he asked me if I would be singing on the show.

I said, "Mr. Roy, I don't sing. I'm a comedian."

"Oh, you are?" he said. "Are you as funny as Minnie Pearl?"

I said, "Nobody's as funny as Minnie Pearl."

He smiled back at me. "You're a smart boy," he said.

BIRMINGHAM, BRUCE AYERS, AND MY BROTHER

Family keeps you humble. Well—maybe not yours, but mine does. Every once in a while, one of them will ask me where I'm headed the next week. I'll tell 'em and they'll say, "Well, be careful," and that'll be it. That has long been the extent of their interest in comedy, and that's fine with me, actually. We didn't talk about my business any more than we talked about my brother's business. He was a plumber.

My family has always loved going to Cracker Barrel. (We're usually at the one at Highway 138 and I-20 East, Exit 82 in Conyers, Georgia. If you stop in, you might run into us.) To this day it's where I meet my nieces. We always sit at that one big round table that every Cracker Barrel has in the corner, the one that holds eight people.

At one point, people began to recognize me and they'd come by the table to say hello. They'd apologize for interrupting—no problem, I'd say—then they'd ask me to sign something or take a picture, and then they'd ask about who else was at the table. This is where my mother would point to my brother. "This is my other son. He's a plumber—he's the Super Plumber!" It was true, by the way. He called himself "Super Plumber." My mother made sure her plumber son got just as much attention as her comedian son. Then he'd give them his business card. On the back, it said, "Your shit is my bread and butter."

I admired my brother greatly. We were very close. My family does not generally come see me perform, which is fine with me, but my brother would come out pretty often, especially when I was working at Bruce Ayers's comedy club in Birmingham.

In the early part of 2003, my brother was diagnosed with bladder cancer. The doctors told us he might make it eighteen months, but we weren't going to settle for that. He made several trips to Cancer Treatment Centers of America in Zion, Illinois. Later, he received outstanding care closer to home at the Winship Cancer Institute of Emory University Hospital. He made it way beyond the eighteen months they gave him. In fact, he made it seven years. My brother passed away in November 2010.

The Emory University Hospital has been good to my family. They took care of my brother, of course. They also took good care of my father in the last few years of his life. And when I had my heart issues, the folks at Emory were there for me, too. These days, I'm over there frequently just to keep up my own health. They're good folks there and I've contributed to the institute and the hospital over the years. They've done so much for me and mine, up to and including saving my life. How could you not want to pay it forward?

When my brother passed away, we had a very small, very private service. It wasn't in a church but in a chapel, and only for family. This is the way we do funerals in the Gregory family, always have. I was sitting on the front porch of the funeral home when I looked up to see Bruce Ayers and his wife Che Che. They had driven over 150 miles from their home in Birmingham.

***

I could write a book about the comedy club, later known as the Stardome, in Birmingham, Alabama, the owner, Bruce Ayers, and his wife and partner, Che Che. Instead of writing a book on this subject, I'll just summarize my relationship with Bruce and the forty years we've known each other. It's important to me and I want you to know about it.

The Punchline in Atlanta opened in 1982. The following year, a few other comedy clubs opened in the Carolinas, Alabama, and Tennessee. The first show at the club in Birmingham featured me, Rob Cleveland, and John Mendoza, the headliner. From that moment till now, I have performed every six months in Birmingham. When I'm headed to Birmingham, it doesn't feel like I'm going to work. It feels like I'm going to visit family and friends. Bruce and Che Che have become family to me.

Bruce is one of those rare individuals who is always upbeat, always positive, and there is no negativity, no gossip. At this point in our lives, we rarely discuss comedy or business. We both know that I'll be working there every six months till I die or he retires. These days, our conversation is about family and friends, things like "How's your niece doing?" and "What's that nephew of yours up to?"—you know. The things that matter most.

Bruce and Che Che still talk about my brother. From the time I'm sitting here writing this, it's been thirteen years since my brother passed. He loved the Stardome comedy club. He could drive fifteen miles to see my show at the Punchline in Atlanta, but instead he'd drive 160 miles to see my show in Birmingham. Bruce treated my brother like royalty. He would even reserve a parking spot for my brother right at the front door—set it up with an orange cone! My brother soaked it up. The memory still makes me smile.

I was sitting in a rocking chair on the porch of the funeral home just before my brother's service was to begin when I looked up and saw Bruce and Che Che coming up the steps. Before I could say anything, Bruce said, "I had to be here." Bruce and I have shared a lot of laughs together over the years, as well as some tears along the way. If Bruce is ever in jail—ha, like that could happen—or in the ICU, I want him to know I'll be there, and the first thing he'll hear me say is, "I had to be here."

After the graveside ceremony with just family, I gave him a call to see if he wanted to join us for lunch. He said they were headed to the Waffle House. I told him he should come with us instead to Golden Corral. "Shame on you, James Gregory," he said. "You know why we are at the Waffle House? Your brother loved the Waffle House. What are you doing at the Golden Corral?" Minutes earlier, I had been weeping. Now Bruce had me laughing.

Bruce was the first club owner to book me as a headliner. He started out with a country music nightclub downtown, then added comedy one weekend a month. I remember how over the years, Bruce would take me to radio stations in the morning to promote the show, and we'd stop to have breakfast and talk about what was ahead. We wondered if this comedy business would work out. We wondered if there was a future in what we were doing. Things worked out for me, as you know. And Bruce's little experiment with comedy quickly grew into one of the most prestigious comedy rooms in America.

Also, for a while, his club was one of the most famous, but for a reason he'd rather forget.

In March 1993, Carrot Top, whose real name is Scott Thompson, was starting to get some attention as a "prop comic."

For his entire act, he pulls props out of trunks and makes jokes with them. He would go on to be a record-setting resident headliner in Las Vegas, but at this time he was building his reputation. Scott was headlining in Birmingham in the middle of that month when a giant snowstorm hit—twenty inches on the ground. That's a lot for any place, but for Birmingham being so far south, it was historic. The snow shut down the city. Bruce closed the club for the storm but, so the story goes, someone in the kitchen left a rag near a fryer, which started a fire. That fire burned not only the comedy club, but also the entire strip mall it was in.

The fire burned up all of Carrot Top's props. He was set to do the Leno show and that had to be postponed, an unthinkable setback for any comedian. But Bruce's problem was even worse: he lost the way he and all his employees made a living, plus the comedians who were booked there in the coming weeks. He was sitting at home watching TV when they interrupted programming. He sat on his couch and saw his club was burning to the ground. With all that snow, he had to catch a ride with a TV news crew to get there.

He didn't stay closed for long. Until he could rebuild, Bruce set up a temporary club in a hotel lounge just outside of the city. The idea, of course, was to keep the staff employed, to honor the gigs with the performers, and to get Bruce the money he needed to rebuild. He called me and asked me to come perform. I consider Bruce a true friend, so of course I wanted to do all I could. We planned for the usual nine-show week, but the outpouring was so great that we ended up doing seventeen shows, including a Saturday where we did one show every two hours starting at three in the afternoon.

Never before or since have I done seventeen shows in a week. Neither had Bruce. In fact, he told me that when he tells other comedians and club owners about doing seventeen shows in six days, they think he's lying. But it's the truth, and he deserved such a good outcome. Bruce is one of those special people. He and his wife—and Birmingham—mean the world to me.

***

Bruce always looks out for me. For example, there are a few clubs where you can't sell merchandise in the lobby. You have to sell it outside. Bruce's club was one of those, so that meant I'd be outside after the show. On one occasion, I was working his club in November and it was cold. Something about me is I never wear a coat. I just don't like it. But Bruce was afraid I'd catch a cold without one. He'd come out to try to get me to wear one but I'd always say no. "Christmas is next month," he said to the other comedians. "Can't y'all buy this man a coat?"

They already knew the answer. "He won't wear it!" they said.

After the Thursday night show, I went outside as usual but this time I found that my friend Bruce had set up a portable outdoor heater, six feet tall, with an extension cord extending down the sidewalk. "That's your heater," he said. "So you won't get cold." That was about forty years ago, but to this day he's worried about me getting cold. "You have on an undershirt? At least put on an undershirt!"

I've been fortunate to encounter kind people wherever I go. My family is buried in the cemetery at Turner Hill Baptist Church on Turner Hill Road, a bit outside the city limits of Lithonia. When it came to my sister's funeral, the people at the funeral home asked if I'd like a special accompaniment on the ride to the cemetery, since the Lithonia police couldn't escort us beyond the city limits. They would clear the way for us at all the intersections, including getting us across Interstate 20. I thought that sounded like a good idea, and sure enough, these two gentlemen, one a retired policeman, rode along with the procession in front and back.

It just goes to show that there are good people everywhere, thoughtful people. When I get down about the future of the country, I remind myself that if you choose to be nice to people, good things happen. Warren "Rhubarb" Jones was the longest-running morning radio DJ in the history of Atlanta. I met him when he was at a station in Alabama. He put me on the air, which is always a good thing in my business, and I came to admire him greatly. After he got out of the radio business, he got involved in adult education and eventually became a faculty member at Kennesaw State University in Kennesaw, Georgia. His title was "distinguished lecturer of mass communications." It was through Rhubarb that I found out about an unfilled need among the students there.

Turns out a college scholarship is not a free ride. Kids still need to buy books and supplies and they still have living expenses. A scholarship doesn't generally cover those things. Rhubarb helped me establish a scholarship for kids there to help fill the gap, so they could spend more time studying and less time working at one or two or even three part-time jobs. These are impressive young people, too. I hear from them occasionally and it's always "Yes, sir," and "No, sir," which are things I say myself. I believe when you encounter young people who are thoughtful in this way, it's a pretty good sign they're going places.

I'd never have known about this need if my friend Rhubarb hadn't opened that door for all of us.

THE FREEDOM TO SAY
WHAT'S ON YOUR MIND

I love this great country of ours, but lately I'm very concerned for my nieces, my nephews, their kids, and their kids' kids. I'm starting to doubt they will get to experience the best of what our country has been. And just because I've been around a few years doesn't mean I'm pining for some version of the 1950s. What's changed about America has happened only in the past few years.

There have always been words we don't say because they're hurtful or wrong. You know what those words are. But we've always supported people's right to express their opinion about things, even when that opinion is controversial. *Sticks and stones may break my bones but words will never hurt me*—that's how we taught kids from early on.

That's changed.

As somebody who talks for a living, I feel pretty strongly that you ought to be able to say what's on your mind and not get pushed out of society over it. But a lot of people now say that we should forbid not only certain words, but also a whole lot of ideas.

It's a dark day when you have to be careful what you say in even a private conversation for fear of somebody whipping up a mob on the internet to get you fired over it.

Yes, some opinions make people uncomfortable, but if we start "canceling" people for sharing their ideas, how are we going to figure out what we believe? And who gets to decide what you can say and what you can't? Right now, all somebody has to say is that they're offended, then get up an anonymous mob to go along. That is wrong, wrong, wrong. Even a bank robber gets a trial.

We have to be able to discuss and debate freely—as the wrestlers say, no holds barred. The price of that is that sometimes, people are going to have their feelings hurt. Seems to me that's a pretty good trade-off for getting to say what you think, getting to hear what other people think, and seeing that we can live together anyway.

This "cancel culture" thing is nothing more than a way for a few people to get their way by making the price of disagreement too high for anyone to pay. If you want to defeat an idea, defeat it with your better idea.

***

If things are going to get better, and I hope they will, it's going to have to come from the young people. They are entitled to figure out the world on their own and make mistakes while they're doing it—but they have to allow that from other people, too. I was wrong about a lot of things when I was young. It just took me a while to figure it out. The problem today is they have been taught to assume that everyone who came before, and anyone who disagrees with them, is not just wrong but evil.

How about this: Everybody who ever lived has done good things and bad things. Why don't we praise them for the good things, and try not to repeat the bad things? God help us if a hundred years from now somebody's gonna go through our lives and condemn us forever for what we got wrong.

Most of what I've learned in life has come from the mistakes I've made. One thing I've learned is that facts are more important than feelings. Wishing doesn't making anything so. That's why I rejected a "dream" long ago in favor of a goal! Another is that we can't all have our own "truth." We can draw our own conclusions about, say, a car accident, but how we feel doesn't change what happened at the intersection. Here's another: if you want to get ahead in life tomorrow, you're going to have to sacrifice today. Maybe that means saving money and doing without. Maybe it means studying more and going out less, or living in somebody's basement instead of a nicer apartment. Or, like me, maybe it means moving back in with your parents and sleeping in the back of your car while you're pursuing the career you want for your life.

For years, we could trust our schools to pass along these ideas that most of us hold in common. But a small minority is betraying the trust of parents and citizens by telling kids that what they learn at home is wrong. Most young adults have spent their entire time in school being told that this country is evil right down to its founding. Thank goodness for those teachers who refuse to go along.

It must be hard to be a young person when the loudest message you hear is that you are oppressed. We used to teach our children, "You can do anything!" Now they learn that they are helpless to build a good life because someone, somewhere is holding them down. It must feel terrible. The only thing worse is to be the child who is taught he's an oppressor, and that he's not entitled to have a good life or feel good about himself. He's told his ancestors were evil and that now he has to pay for it.

No matter what kids hear these days, this much is still true: while we don't all start in the same place, we are all entitled to take our best shot at creating the life we want. Decent people treat everybody the same. We ought to look past skin color and religion and all that, not start with it.

Humor can help get us through a lot of things, even the toughest things. I grew up with black friends and white friends, we got along, and there was no tension between us. Part of that was because we shared our sense of humor.

My sister had a good friend named Gerri, a black woman who was one of our family's greatest friends. My sister and I used to get together once a week for dinner at a little buffet place in Tucker, Georgia. One day, Gerri was there, too, and on a diet. While I was digging into the fried chicken and mashed potatoes, she stuck with the salad bar. When the waitress came by, Gerri told her there weren't any crackers. "I can't eat without crackers," Gerri said.

The waitress pointed at me and my sister and said, "You're eating with two crackers right now!" We all sat there and laughed and laughed at that silly joke. So did the people sitting around us. Some were black, some were white. We laughed together. Those were better days.

***

Did you ever think you'd live long enough to see people tear down statues to commemorate great men of American history? In some cities, they've renamed things named after George Washington, who risked everything he had to establish this country, and

BACKSTAGE GETTING READY TO GO ON STAGE AT THE HUDSON THEATRE IN HOLLYWOOD, CA

CARROT TOP & DEAN GAINES AT MY CHRISTMAS PARTY

HUDSON THEATRE SET—HOLLYWOOD, CA

JAMES & BROTHER MELVIN (1959 IN FRONT OF HOUSE IN LITHONIA, GEORGIA)

JAMES GREGORY PROMO PIC

ME & BRIAN DORFMAN (OWNER OF ZANIES IN NASHVILLE)

ME & CARROT TOP AT MY YEARLY CHRISTMAS PARTY

ME & DENNIS HOPPER AND UNKNOWN WOMAN

ME & DAN MENGINI AT NASHVILLE
SCHERMERHORN SYMPHONY HALL
BEFORE A SHOW

MARY EMMA (SISTER) &
"WHISPERING" BILL ANDERSON

ME & CLOSE FRIEND VINNIE COPPOLA

ME & DUSTY RHODES

ME & KENNY CHESNEY ON HIS BUS FOR HIS NYE SHOW 2002

ME & MANY COMEDIANS AT MY ANNUAL CHRISTMAS PARTY. BACK ROW FROM LEFT TO RIGHT: JIM BRICK, KEN SONS, DARYL PINSKY, DEAN GAINES, REX GARVIN, ME (JAMES), GREG RAY, CHARLES VIRACOLA, CHRIS TITUS, STEVE PLEMMONS, JIM HANNA; (MIDDLE ROW) JOBY SAAD, STEVE MINGOLLA; (BOTTOM ROW) MARK DICHIARA, CARROT TOP, TIM WILSON, PAM & LES MCCURDY

ME & MY MANAGER, LENNY SISSELMAN DURING OPERATION ENDURING FREEDOM (2002)

ME & NANCY (GEORGE) JONES BACK-
STAGE AT GRAND OLE OPRY

ME AND ONE OF MY FAVORITE
PEOPLE BRUCE AYERS (OWNER
OF THE STARDOME)

ME & NED BEATTY

ME & RICKY VAN SHELTON

ME & STEVE MINGOLLA

ME AT TEN YEARS OLD (1956)

ME ABOUT TO TAKE OFF ON HELICOPTER
DURING OPERATION ENDURING FREEDOM
(NOT VERY EXCITED AS I AM SURE YOU
CAN TELL)

ME AT MY CLASSIC MERCH TABLE

ME ON STAGE AT ONE OF MY MANY (100'S) CORPORATE SHOWS

ME ON THE WAY TO PERFORM ON THE USS VELLA GULF CRUISE (2002)

ME PERFORMING ON THE TEDDY ROOSEVELT AIRCRAFT CARRIER (2002)

ME PERFORMING ON THE USS OGDEN FOR 500+ SAILORS & MARINES (2002)

ME SHOOTING A 50 CALIBER MACHINE GUN ON THE AIRCRAFT CARRIER (2002)

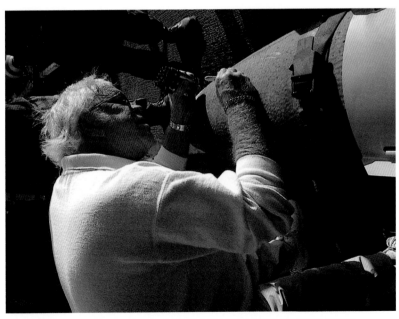

ME SIGNING A BOMB MEANT FOR OSAMA BIN LADEN WHILE ON THE TEDDY ROOSEVELT AIRCRAFT CARRIER IN THE INDIAN OCEAN (2002)

ME WITH A CAMEL IN BAHRAIN (2002)

ME WITH KEITH BILBREY & LARRY BLACK AT "LARRY'S COUNTRY DINER" TAPING

MELVIN (BROTHER) & ME (EARLY 2000S)

MELVIN (BROTHER), ME & MARY EMMA (SISTER)—1967

MELVIN (JAMES' BROTHER), WILLIE BELL GREGORY (JAMES' MOMMA), JAMES HAROLD GREGORY, SR (JAMES' DAD) AND ME (LITHONIA, GEORGIA 1963)

MY FAMILY PIC: ME, DAD, MELVIN (BROTHER), MOMMA & MARY EMMA (SISTER)

MY CLASSIC CARICATURE THAT
I USED FOR PROMO MY ENTIRE
CAREER

MY FAMOUS PROMO SHOT

RON DINUNZIO, ME & DAVE MONTESANTO (ORIGINAL OWNERS OF THE
PUNCHLINE IN ATLANTA)

ON SET AT THE HUCKABEE SHOW

JAMES GREGORY

"The Funniest Man In America"

THIS IS THE SIGNED HEADSHOT SENT TO THOUSANDS OF PEOPLE AROUND THE WORLD

TWO OF MY FAVORITE THINGS: CIGARETTES AND COFFEE AT AMSTERDAM AIRPORT (2002)

Abraham Lincoln, who gave his life ending slavery. They deserve our respect and our gratitude.

I think we all have to stand together on this, whatever our race, whatever our religion. It's like Benjamin Franklin said, "We must all hang together, or, most assuredly, we shall all hang separately." I am certain there is more that unites us than divides us, which brings me to a little thing that happened to me years ago, and a nice way to close this out.

One of the clubs I've worked consistently over the years has been Comedy Off Broadway in Lexington, Kentucky. The man who ran the club was Jeff Gilstrap, who as I mentioned, has now passed away. I miss him. Jeff loved comedy, knew a lot about it, and when it came to the comedy business, there was not any daylight between us. He wanted the audience to get more than just a night of jokes. He wanted them to get a real theatrical experience, a show. Me too.

There was one difference between Jeff and me, though. I'm to the Right on most things, but he was to the Left on everything, and he'd let you know it. I remember when a couple of comedians put together a double act they called "The Wiseguys." Jeff wouldn't put up their poster because it had a gun on it. Not only did Jeff not like guns, he didn't even like pictures of guns!

But one of the many things we did agree on was that you have to treat comedy like a business, including promotion. To that end, he would get up in the mornings and drive comedians from the condo to the various radio stations in town so they could promote the show. He didn't want to find out a comedian had been "too tired" to get there, so he'd get up at 5 a.m. and take them himself.

On this particular afternoon, he had booked me for two radio stations. He was in the mood for a nap, and he was fine if I went by myself—he knew I took promotion as seriously as he did.

This being autumn in Kentucky, the radio interview eventually got around to deer season, which was only a few weeks away. The host asked me if I liked to hunt. "Oh, no," I said. "I can't imagine shooting a deer. Or a squirrel! Or a puppy!"

"But you own guns," he said.

"That's right, sir, I do," I said.

"So what do you own guns for?"

"To shoot people!" I said. They busted out laughing.

When I came back, Jeff was waiting for me. "You damn right-wingers!" he said. "You'll shoot a human being but you won't shoot a deer? Is that who I'm dealing with?"

I laughed. "Yes, it is."

He laughed, too. "Damn you. Well, James, I love you anyway." And the fact is that I loved him, too.

I care strongly about our country, but I care just as much about people. Whether you're my close friend or someone I'll never cross paths with, I believe with all my heart that you are important in this world and a child of God, whatever god you believe in. You may not agree with everything I think, but that's fine with me. We don't have to agree on anything except to be respectful of each other and to be friends.

As long as we can talk, we're on the right track. It's a choice, you know: choose to be kind, choose to be forgiving, and choose to be patient.

If we do that, I think we'll be okay. With that in place, surely we can figure out the rest.

Here's the Story: Gym Memberships

"If I give you part of my hard-earned money, will you let me come in here after work every day and lift something heavy?"

I came up with this bit many years ago, back in what I call the "condo years" when I was working my way up. This was long before anybody had a cell phone, too. As usual, I was out with the other comedians after the show, just hanging out and talking. At some point, I guess, one of us said something about getting together for lunch the next day. There was a local comedian with us—I truly don't remember who it was, or even where we were. Anyway, he already had some plans for the next day. He was excited 'cause he had just signed up for a gym membership. He had gotten a deal on the price, some kind of special. I said the first thing I thought of.

"It oughta be free," I said. "'Cause you can just lift something heavy at home."

As it happened so often, that one little remark grew into a longer piece built out of things I thought up on stage or made up and added. That includes the part about finding a businessman who'd let you pay him for the privilege of picking up heavy things. The businessman is all for that good deal. "Yeah," he says. "You got any stupid friends you can bring with you?"

SUPPORTING OUR TROOPS
AFTER 9/11

There's a long tradition of entertainers stepping up to put on a show for soldiers overseas. It's a way to build morale, of course. And for those of us in show business, it's a way to personally say thanks to these men and women who are risking their lives for the rest of us.

Less than a month after 9/11, President Bush ordered military action in the Middle East and Afghanistan. The country was united more than it's been before or since, and a whole lot of singers, actors, and comedians stepped up right away to do what they could to support the troops. A couple of the first comedians asked to make the trip to that part of the world were Jay Leno and Drew Carey. The government reached out to others, too, including me. I am honored that they gave me the opportunity. I was proud to say yes. I had an unforgettable time while I was over there.

But the trip over? That was a different story. It was unforgettable in a different way!

Except for a few shows in Canada, this was my first trip outside the United States, first trip overseas. To get to the Middle East, you have to take a twenty-hour flight. I do not like to fly, and that's putting it mildly. Let's say it scares the hell out of me, how about that? Plus, at the time, I was a heavy smoker, and you couldn't smoke on a plane.

I wasn't just up a creek without a paddle. I was up a creek without a cigarette.

If they could've knocked me out and woke me up when we landed, that would have been fine. Fortunately, I am a world champion at taking a nap.

First, we flew ten hours to Amsterdam. We slept there overnight, then we stretched our legs a little in the city in the morning before heading back to the airport for the eight-hour flight on to the Kingdom of Bahrain, which turns out to be an island in Western Asia at the edge of the Persian Gulf. Bahrain is quite a place. They had signs along the road like back home, except they didn't say "Deer Crossing." They said, "Camel Crossing." I didn't expect that—and that's a true story.

From there, we flew to the USS *Teddy Roosevelt*, an aircraft carrier that holds about five thousand three hundred people. It's like a city, only it floats on the water, and it's an amazing thing. For the next ten days, it would be our home base. They'd take us by helicopter to other ships where I'd do my show. But getting to that ship the first time was scary!

We were coming from Bahrain, landing on the carrier. A normal takeoff and landing strip at an airport is about a half mile long, but on a carrier the pilot has only four hundred feet, about one-sixth of what's normal. When you land, they stop the plane from sailing into the water by catching it on hook against a wire. And when you hit that wire at full speed? Let me tell you, friend, we braced ourselves and still got jerked back into that seat harder than anything you can imagine. At the end of our ten days, when we had to take off, they did the same thing in reverse: they made it like a catapult and flung us into the air.

***

The guys who had been there just before me were legendary athletes, the basketball stars Artis Gilmore and Spud Webb. They came over to visit with the soldiers, give a talk here and there, and to encourage the men and women in uniform, let 'em know how much we appreciated them back home. I was pleased to get to do that, too, plus my show on top of it.

I liked doing the shows—I always do—but I think what meant the most to the military folks was the company. I spent more time hanging out with the soldiers and enjoying their company than I did doing my act. It was obvious they liked just shooting the bull with someone who was interested in what they do, who cared enough to make the trip, and who respected the hard and dangerous work they had signed up for. And make no mistake, this was high-risk work for them in a high-risk place. Every place we went, there were bomb-sniffing dogs. To keep them and us safe, no one could tell us in advance where we were going. Sometimes we didn't know until we got there.

These were outstanding men and women, the cream of the crop. Brave as hell, too—it's easy to forget how scary the world was at that time, less than a year after that son of a bitch Osama bin Laden knocked down the Twin Towers and crashed two more planes filled with innocent people. Back in America, everybody was on edge for the next few years, yet these people in the military were running headfirst into the danger—and doing it on our behalf. A lot of them volunteered to be there. So spending time with them was an honor. It was the least I could do to thank them. I was glad the government gave me the opportunity to do it.

As for the shows, I hadn't worked in any situation quite like it, and I'm sure I never will again. On some of the largest ships, I'd do my show out in the open, on deck. There might be two thousand people out there. Planes were taking off and landing all the time, so it was loud, too. But to be in that place was just flat-out amazing, surrounded by billions of dollars of the most advanced military aircraft in the history of man. And it was the people that made it all work.

Whenever we'd get where we were going, usually to a cruiser, a battleship, a destroyer, or an aircraft carrier, the people we met always made it worth the trip. Someone was assigned to accompany us and to answer all our questions, so on every ship, I'd ask for a tour. They were glad to do it—proud to. On the *Teddy Roosevelt* aircraft carrier, we would stand on the bridge to watch extended maneuvers with F-16s and JF-17s practicing for the long flight to Afghanistan, working side by side with reconnaissance planes and refueler planes to make sure they got back. It was amazingly choreographed, almost like a dance, but with massive airplanes!

The shows I did there took place on the Indian Ocean—and it's like glass, so pretty. At night, there's no light except what comes from the stars, and I could see a million of them. It was fascinating. It was beautiful. It was amazing.

Another time, we were on the nuclear guided-missile cruiser USS *Vella Gulf*, which was the first ship to go around Manhattan after the Twin Towers went down. A young man was showing us row after row of missiles, which would soon be used in combat. This kid was serious about his business—he was *on*, if you know what I mean. So impressive. He knew everything about these massive weapons, which I found stunning for someone so young. I asked him his age. "I'm nineteen, sir," he told me. Then I asked him this: if President Bush gave the command to fire a nuclear weapon from this ship, who would be the one doing it?

The kid didn't hesitate. "That'd be me, sir."

These were all amazing vessels run by amazing people, right down to this young man who was ready to be the tip of the spear. I was in awe.

WHAT'S WORSE THAN A HELICOPTER FLIGHT IN A WAR ZONE?

E very morning, I'd start the day with the crew, usually down in
the smoking pit. At some point, my manager would come over
to tell me what time we were leaving to do my show and where
they'd take us. On this day, Lenny came over to the pit as usual, but
he had something different to tell me. He pointed over the water.
Usually, the Indian Ocean is smooth as glass. That day, it wasn't.

"See that?" he said. It was a ship in the distance. "We're going
over there to perform this afternoon. But it's really windy, so we're
not taking a helicopter."

That was good news to me. Those helicopter trips were even
scarier than the long flight over from the US. At least on an airplane they close the doors. On a military helicopter, I'd sit across
from somebody else, knee to knee, while another guy with his legs
hanging out of the open door sat there manning a machine gun, all
of us just barely a thousand feet over the ocean.

Friends, I did not enjoy those helicopter rides. So if the plan that day was anything else, I figured that was good news. I was wrong, wrong, wrong.

"So how are we getting there?" I said.

"Well, James," he said, and he hesitated, 'cause he knew I wasn't gonna like this next part. "See that rubber raft over there?" he said. It was what's called a RHIB boat, a rigid hull inflatable boat. It was hanging in the air, over the water, off wires or ropes or something, and it was attached to some kind of crane. I must have looked scared already because the dozen guys standing with me started laughing.

"You know, Lenny," I said, "before I had management, I didn't have this kind of problem."

We were headed for the *Whidbey Island*, a dock-landing ship that transports landing craft to and from a beach. The brave men and women on board would soon serve with honor in support of Operation Enduring Freedom, where they would go on to set the record for the longest amphibious operation in American history of nearly seven hundred nautical miles inland. But first we had to get there. That started with, somehow, getting in it.

Let me set the scene for you. We were on the edge of a destroyer about six stories over the ocean, which was like standing on the edge of a building and looking down at concrete. The guy in charge of us gave us a choice. "We can put you in it right here and then lower you down, or we can put the boat in the water and you can climb down a rope ladder," he said.

That was an easy choice. Climb down a six-story rope ladder over the open sea on a windy day? Nope. I told 'em I'd climb in up here and let them lower me down. So that's what they did. It was me, Lenny, our luggage, plus a life vest and a pair of goggles each. It took about ten minutes for them to crank us down. It was our job not to fall out. Since there were no seatbelts, we held on to some rope looped along the side. Friends, I have not held on so tight to anything in my life.

As soon as we hit the water, the thing slammed against the side of the ship and a giant wave washed over us, too. The people who were there tell me that at this point my eyes were as big as dinner plates. I believe them.

As soon as we were in the water, we were on our way. We set out for the other ship but unlike the helicopter trip, we had two gunners, one in the front and one in the back, which doesn't exactly give a man confidence. You'd think being on the water might make you safer from attack than being up in the air, but I guess not.

So we were tearing across the Indian Ocean because they didn't want us exposed any longer than we had to be. About halfway there, I got to thinking: *Getting in this rubber boat had me coming down six stories. How in the world are they gonna get me out of it?* That's when it hit me: I was gonna have to climb back up!

At this time, I was a guy smoking three packs of cigarettes a day. I like to say that I would have smoked four—but I didn't have time.

Now they wanted me to climb a rope ladder swinging out over the ocean—while it was banging against the steel hull of a warship—and I was gonna get whipped back and forth while doing it. This did not strike me as a well-thought-out plan.

But we didn't have a choice. I went first and Lenny came up behind me, and he was carrying the luggage. (It's still a mystery to me why they didn't haul it up with the boat.) He was carrying this stuff like he was Jerry Lewis in *The Bellboy*, a few feet behind me, shimmying up this ladder that was whipping in the wind, sometimes swinging out in the open air and sometimes hugging up against the hull. If you picture it, you'll realize that these kinds of ships get narrower toward the water, so basically when we were not whipping around like a carnival ride, we were climbing up at about a forty-five-degree angle, leaning back.

And I made it! To this day, I have no idea how. I already had heart issues, but I didn't know it yet. I was extremely overweight. But I got through it anyway. Maybe it was adrenaline? Maybe I just didn't want to let it beat me. Either way, as soon as I got up on deck, I fell out, just collapsed on my back, trying to catch my breath. I didn't know I had it in me!

A minute later, Lenny came up to where I was spread out. I was beat and out of breath, but I had one question for him, a question I had to ask before I could go on.

"Lenny," I said, "where's the smoking pit?"

A LOT OF TROUBLE FOR
A LOT OF GOLD

L et me tell you something about me that you may not know: I like nice things. I like gold jewelry, good furniture, beautiful things on the wall. Maybe it's because I grew up without too much and now I'm making up for it. Who knows? All I know is I enjoy having nice things.

Turns out that if you want to buy gold, Bahrain is the place to be. There aren't any duties on gold there so you can get quite a deal, plus the workmanship is some of the best in the world. When we first arrived, Lenny and I went to a huge mall called Gold City filled with gold dealers and craftsmen. Inside, they had dozens of little stores where they sold diamonds, pearls, precious stones, and precious metals. But mostly they sold gold—everywhere you looked, gold, and jewelry designers and craftsmen who could make anything you could think up. I talked to some jewelers and had them make some custom pieces for me to pick up when we finished the trip. We came back to pick up the gold. It should have been simple, but it wasn't.

It was the afternoon and I decided to stay in my room and take a nap. Lenny said he would walk over there and pick up the stuff for both of us. He'd be gone an hour at most.

Our hotel was about five blocks from Gold City, which takes up an entire city block. The mall itself was a perfect square, and every entrance looked exactly the same, with a dozen granite steps that take you up inside. Lenny walked in there around three in the afternoon, plenty of time to get back to the hotel before the sun went down around four thirty. He picked out what he thought was a unique landmark, a steeple on a mosque—a minaret, it's called. That way he'd know he was leaving by the same door he came in.

Turns out when you're in a Muslim country, choosing a minaret for a landmark is like picking a cornfield for a landmark in Tennessee. When he came out of the mall, he left by a different door, and there was a minaret you could see from there. It looked just like the one from when he came in, but it was a different one.

So he was walking the wrong way.

There's no good time to get lost in a foreign country, but this time was definitely a lot worse than others. To sum it up, my manager, a Jew in a Muslim country just after 9/11, was lost, wandering around a city he'd never seen, among people he didn't know who spoke a language he'd never heard, the day before the weekly Muslim day of prayer when everything shuts down, the sun was setting—and he was carrying around $10,000 in gold.

After a while being lost, he was desperate to find anything familiar. At one point, he thought he was walking back toward the mall but he wasn't. In fact, he was walking into a residential neighborhood—no stores, no business, just people living their lives. It was clear that this guy in blue jeans and a polo shirt did not belong there. People were cooking outside and of course no one was speaking English—why would they?—and he just wanted to get back to the hotel. At this point, off in the distance he saw a Kentucky Fried Chicken restaurant, and he remembered that there was one of those across from the hotel. Maybe this one was that one? But as he approached it, he realized it wasn't the same restaurant after all.

Now it was dark, and somehow he had walked to the beach. (The country of Bahrain is a tiny island. Unless he walked in circles, he had to hit the beach some time.) He figured that this would eventually lead him back to the hotel because the hotel is on the beach. Even if he had to walk around most of the island— most of the country—he'd still get there.

And that's what happened. He got back safe and sound—and with all the gold. It had been a trip of close to three hours—to return from a mall ten minutes away. He called me when he got back. "James, I'm a basket case," he said. I could believe that. He told me the story, brought the gold by the room, and we counted our blessings that things turned out okay.

If you're gonna get hurt during a war in the Middle East, you figure it'll be because you wandered into the action, not because you took a wrong turn at Kentucky Fried Chicken. We were both ready to go home. Other than that scary detour at the end of it for my friend, it was one of the most rewarding trips of my life.

Here's the Story: Flotation Seat

"There's no ocean between Atlanta and Los Angeles. You wanna make me happy, show me a seat that's gonna bounce out of a cornfield."

Where did this one come from? That was just my brilliance. It just came to me. Ha!

Actually this is one of the oldest bits I do. It's the truth; I really don't like to fly. Wherever it is I have to go, I drive. The only reason I'll fly is if I have to be there and there's no time to get there any other way. Other than that, I'm fine with a car ride.

I'm just telling you the truth. If you're at thirty thousand feet and something comes off, you can't pull over and see what it is. They know it's not safe because they brag about their safety features, especially that seat that floats if they make an emergency landing…in the ocean. But if I'm taking off in Georgia and landing in California, flying completely over land every mile—well, I don't think a flotation device is gonna save me.

HOW ABOUT MAYONNAISE
ON A PIZZA?

A couple of years after my trip to the Middle East, I had the honor of being invited to entertain the troops again. This time they sent me to Italy, Greece, and Spain. The difference was that this time they didn't send me to a war zone. That made it a whole lot easier.

Also on this trip, I learned something new. Before I went to Spain, I did not know that you could put mayonnaise on a pizza. Turns out that you can. I didn't think anybody would want to, but they do. Over in Spain it's a different story.

I was on this trip with Steve Mingolla, a comedian they call the "Nice Guy of Comedy." We were in a restaurant with the same kind of setup as they have back home at IHOP or Waffle House, with containers on the table for fixing up your food: a red container for ketchup, a yellow one for mustard, and like that. While Steve and I were waiting for our order, a couple came in and ordered pizza. When it came out, it sure looked good. Steve and I decided we should have ordered that instead, but then something else happened. These two people reached over to those little plastic containers. They picked up the white one and smeared whatever was in it all over that pizza.

I asked Steve what it was. "Mayonnaise!" he said.

"On pizza?" I said.

Yeah, it was mayonnaise. Turns out Spanish people like it on a lot of stuff—maybe everything.

After our meal came, we noticed an older couple sitting not far from us. They were eating something—it looked like a big burger, but it wasn't. Maybe it was another pizza. Anyway, when it came, they took the top off that white container and started smearing mayonnaise all over their food, too. It didn't look good to me or to Steve. For the rest of our time in Spain, we made jokes about mayonnaise.

Fast-forward fifteen years later. I'm in a QuikTrip convenience store, a QT they call it. You've been in a place like that so you know that they have a place where you can get a hot dog and fix it up your own way with mustard and relish and all that. I had come in the store to pay for my gas and to get a Dr. Pepper fountain drink. I was also thinking I might like a chicken sandwich or a hot dog, too. There were a lot of day laborers in this QT. Some of them were getting hot dogs and fixing 'em up the way I would. But then these guys reached over and grabbed a bunch of packets of mayonnaise.

I hollered over at 'em, "Hey! Are you guys from Spain?" Instantly, they all started smiling. They came over and hugged me! One of them asked me how I knew where they came from.

"It was easy. You put that awful mayonnaise on your hot dog!"

Mayonnaise on a hot dog? Maybe. But I still don't want any mayonnaise on my pizza.

WHEN I'M ON STAGE, I'M TELLING YOU HOW I REALLY FEEL

People ask me, out of all the routines I do, which one is my favorite. The answer depends on when you ask me. That's because my favorite routine is the one the audience laughed at the most that night. When I get a big laugh, that shows me I'm doing my job well.

But I can for sure tell you what I don't like: jokes that aren't really jokes. If you're just saying something the audience likes to cheer for, you're not doing comedy. And the response you get? Bill Maher calls it "clapter," meaning the audience is clapping and hooting in agreement instead of laughing because it's funny. I don't like material that's just to get a response. If it's not funny it's not going to be in my routine, and it doesn't belong in anybody's routine. You can be a comedian or you can be a cheerleader. You can't be both.

These days, the worst of that is Donald Trump jokes. The late-night hosts rarely tell a joke about Donald Trump that's actually a joke. It's just them saying they don't like him and the people in their audience agreeing—more of that "clapter."

I also do not like doing stuff that everybody else is talking about. I call that stuff a "Chicken McNugget joke."

If you listen to the DVD I recorded in Chattanooga, Tennessee in 1985, you'll hear a routine on there about Chicken McNuggets. McDonald's came out with McNuggets a little before then and every comedian was making jokes about them. That included me, though to this day I'm pretty sure I had the funniest routine about them, I really do. But anyway.

I was in a comedy club in Arlington, Texas, in a space in the lobby where comedians would hang out. I was listening to a conversation between the club owner, the local emcee, and some other comedians. The emcee said, "I love being here and I love emceeing. Anytime you need me, I'm available. But you ought to let me be the feature act once in a while. I'm funny enough."

The club owner, who had a gravelly voice and a slow delivery, laid it out for the kid. "Opening act. Middle act. Headliner. There's no big difference. If you're the opening act, you do your Chicken McNugget joke. It gets a smile, maybe a nod. Then the feature shows up with his McNugget joke and all of a sudden that kind of material gets some laughs. Next thing you know the headliner hits the stage with more of the same McNugget stuff and blows the roof off the place. Not much difference between those comedians. Pretty much all the same."

Pretty much all the same. What he said really hit me. For that reason, I never told another Chicken McNugget joke again. It's not enough to get a reaction. If the reaction you get depends only on where you are in the lineup, that's not much of an act. Then and there, I changed. If everybody is talking about something, I don't talk about it at all. Why? My goal is not just to be the funniest comedian up there. I want to be the most original, too. I don't want anyone to hear my act and someone else's act and say *it's pretty much all the same.*

In recent years, my show has changed a bit. These days, there's often a strong message in the things I say. I have to tell you, I'm enjoying it more because of that. But that doesn't mean I'm ignoring what the audience wants in favor of what I prefer. I always have been and always will be up there for the audience, my paying customers. I will say, though, that sometimes when I talk about something with a message, there's more to the audience's reaction than laughter. Maybe they're tired of being told by the news to feel guilty about the environment, or to stop using plastic straws, or to drive a smaller car, or to get rid of your gas stove because somebody else says you have to.

People who come to my show work hard for their money, and they are tired of being told how to live by people who don't know anything of hard work in the real world. Most of us don't have private jets, we don't get paid to tell other people how to live, and we don't have any desire to boss other people around. When someone talks a little common sense from behind the microphone on the comedy stage, that feels good to hear.

***

There's a routine I do that you may have heard, the one about people who get caught in a tornado. I would combine it with a routine about people who saw a UFO, and people who think they saw Elvis, but I concentrated on the part about tornadoes.

I believe there is a conspiracy to make those of us who live in tornado country look ignorant on TV. What are the odds that out of the thousands of tornadoes and destroyed homes, they can never find anybody who's been to the dentist?

I believe with all my heart that when a tornado hits, the news director at the local TV stations tells his reporter, "Get out to the trailer park and interview a dumbass. And try to find one who's married to a fat woman."

Well, around 2011 in Alabama, they had the biggest tornado in the history of the state. A few days after it hit, I was supposed to do a corporate event in Florence, Alabama. Since I live in Georgia, it was just about as quick to drive there as to fly. As usual, I stuck to the state highways, 'cause those are the roads I like—plus the interstate doesn't go there, so it's the only way to drive. On this trip, that route took me up close to some of the horrendous damage that the tornadoes had done. It was horrible. Residential areas were just smashed. Businesses were gone. At one point, I saw a mom with two kids standing by the side of the road with a handmade sign written on cardboard: *Please help. We need fresh water.*

By the time I got to that event, I had made up my mind that I would never do that tornado routine again. I had done that routine for twenty-seven years. It was hysterical. People loved it. Heck, I loved it. I still do. Other comedians make jokes about tornadoes and get big laughs, but I had the funniest routine of all. Yet after what I saw, things changed. That mother and her kids just wanting clean water? It breaks your heart, tears it in two.

In some ways, it was foolish for me to stop doing that bit, like a mechanic throwing away a perfectly good tool. And the truth is that there were times that routine helped people who had gone through the experience. I would go into places that had been hit hard by tornadoes, places like Jackson, Tennessee, for instance. They get hit by tornadoes pretty often. I'd do that routine and people would love it. It was kind of a relief for them, you know. Like *we got hit but we're still standing.*

But what I saw on the way to Florence? It changed me. It wasn't just that I didn't want to do it again. I couldn't do it again, I just couldn't. I can't explain it. Some things just change you. What I say on stage is what I really feel.

A BUSHEL OF BEANS AND A PECK OF TOMATOES

I was born at home, out in the country. When I tell you that, I don't mean we were so far out there that there weren't hospitals. They were there, you just had to a drive a bit to get to them. My brothers and my sister were born in the charity ward of Grady Hospital in Atlanta, because we were poor and it didn't cost anything. I was born at home because I showed up early. I made my first appearance on May 6, 1946, at 4:15 in the afternoon on my mother's kitchen table.

My mother had been through this before and she could tell I was coming fast. When her water broke, it was too late to go to the hospital. The doctor was gonna have to come to us, but we didn't have a phone. The nearest one was down the road at the home of a gentleman named Hiram Stevenson. My father went down there to have him make the call to Old Doctor Stewart—that's what we called him, Old Doctor Stewart. You had to be specific with the name because there was another Doctor Stewart, his son, who had a pharmacy down on Main Street. We called him Younger Doctor Stewart. Anyway, Old Doctor Stewart came right out and it was a good thing because it was a difficult delivery. He took care of my mom and got me birthed.

At that point, all that was left was to settle up the bill. My dad told Old Doctor Stewart that he was grateful for the service, but that he couldn't afford to pay right then, and he'd pay just as soon as he could. In those days, and still to this day, most people around there had a garden out front, sometimes just a few plants, sometimes a plot big as the endzone of a football field. You'd plant your stuff in May and your crops would start coming up in June. Keep in mind, this was May, halfway between planting things and taking them out of the ground. Old Doctor Stewart was a good man, and he told my dad not to worry about the bill.

"Tell ya what," he said. "When your garden comes in, just give me a bushel of beans and a peck of tomatoes, and we'll call it even."

From that day forward, when my dad thought I was a little bit too mischievous, a little too far out of line, he'd call back to what Old Doctor Stewart said on the day I was born.

"Son," he'd say, "don't make me regret that bushel of beans and that peck of tomatoes." I've lived my whole life trying to keep that in mind. I never wanted my dad to regret what he got for that bushel of beans and a peck of tomatoes.

For the most part, I don't believe I disappointed him. I wasn't a saint, but I could have gotten in a lot more trouble than I did. I didn't taste alcohol until I was twenty-three, and I didn't like it. I was a heavy smoker from early on, but that was a lot more common back then, than it is now. Used to be there were cigarette ads where a doctor would recommend the brand he smoked because it was healthier. So I don't think "heavy smoker" was the kind of trouble my daddy was worried about for me. I think I've done all right. Though I did have a close call I'll always remember.

When I was sixteen, we lived on what's called Old Covington Highway, east of downtown Lithonia, Georgia. It's a small town now but back then it was even smaller. One stoplight, that was it. The highway came into town and at the city limits that road was called Swift Street. The first time I got stopped for speeding was right there on Swift, where the speed limit drops at the city limit sign. I got pulled over by an officer by the name of Wallace Moore, who was the chief of police. When I say, "chief of police," keep in mind that there weren't but three cops for the whole town. To keep things covered, each one worked an eight-hour shift. I was in my dad's car, a '53 Ford, because my dad always drove an old car.

I heard that siren go off and I pulled over. Chief Moore came over to the car and asked for my license, looked at it, then looked at me. "Your name is Gregory?" he said. "Which one of those Gregory boys is your daddy?" This was a tiny town where everybody knew everybody else. Everybody knew the name Gregory, and the Gregory boys were my dad and my two uncles.

"Yes, sir," I said. "My dad is Harold Gregory." Then he said something to me I'll never forget.

"I'm not gonna give you a ticket and I'm not gonna tell your daddy," he said. "If I catch you speeding a second time, I still won't give you a ticket. But I *will* call your daddy."

Because of that, I made sure that I never got pulled over again. I was a lot more afraid of my dad than I was a cop, even the chief of police.

It was a different time, and in that way, it was a much better time. You want a sixteen-year-old boy to toe the line in Lithonia, Georgia? Tell him you're gonna talk to his daddy. He'll straighten up right off. I know I did.

***

Those good times come with good feelings that have been with me for the rest of my life, warm feelings for my mom and dad, and how it was to grow up in that place. We didn't have much, as I have said, but we did not want for the love that a parent has for their children. I remember being a teenager and going out for the evening, telling them I might not be back before midnight. They'd tell me that was fine. "We'll keep the porch light on for you." That's what they'd say.

When I started doing comedy, I moved back home for a while. I'd have a weekend show in, say, South Carolina. I'd drive over to do those three shows and wrap up after midnight on Saturday. Since there wasn't a Sunday show, I could drive home afterward, but I'd have to drive all through the night and get in around 4 a.m. Our back door had a screen on it with a latch, so before I'd leave, I'd remind my dad to not put that latch on before he went to bed. I was coming up on forty years old, starting my professional life over again, and I was asking my dad to leave the door open for me when I came home after midnight. I said to my brother that it was like being a teenager again.

But you know, my dad never made me feel bad about that. He cared greatly about what happened to me, and he let me live at home all those years later without making me feel bad for it.

And he never forgot to leave up the latch on that screen door, not one time.

With all my heart, I hope my daddy felt like he got a good deal on what he traded to get me, a bushel of beans and a peck of tomatoes.

Here's the Story: Will Work for Food

"I offered this guy an onion to paint my house. He gave me the finger. So the homeless can be rude!"

"I got an acre of land that needs clearing off. Hop in!" He won't get in.

We've all seen these guys on the corner with the sign, "Will Work for Food." I'm happy to help people in need, but I always suspected that these people weren't sincere, especially when you see the same guy on the same corner year after year. I figure that if you stop and tell one of these people that you need work done on your yard, they're not gonna get in your car for the promise of a hot meal. Somebody said to me, "You don't know. You oughta try that sometime." That gave me the idea for the joke.

I came up with this: I'd say that I rolled the window down and offered this guy a squash to paint my house. That didn't work—I couldn't make it funny. So I kept switching out the vegetable. Then I tried it with "onion"—and that one worked.

Then there's that tagline after the punch line: Hell, it was a Vidalia!

THE TIME I NEARLY DIED

S o far, I've mentioned this only in passing. Now let me tell you the whole story.

In 2004, I nearly died. Seriously. And I'll tell you who saved my life: a cosmetic surgeon.

I've had some cosmetic surgery here and there. Get this or that tucked, get some wrinkles taken away, that sort of thing. I'd have this done in Atlanta. But somebody told me about an especially accomplished cosmetic surgeon in Birmingham by the name of Dr. Paul Howard. Not only was he a great doctor, he was and is a great guy. He and a group of other doctors had created a foundation to do something wonderful: they would rebuild faces and limbs for children who had been injured in a fire or some other catastrophe, and they'd do it at no charge whatsoever.

I made an appointment and told him what little things I wanted done. Then he surprised me with a deal: he said he'd do my work for free if I'd participate in the next fundraiser for their foundation. Well, yeah! I'd happily do a show to raise money to help those children, glad to. It was a great cause and I was pleased to be able to help. Of course we had a deal.

At this point, I had had cosmetic surgery before and I didn't think of these procedures as a big deal. It's not like they were going "inside," you know, so the doctors I'd seen before never asked for any kind of medical testing in advance. Dr. Howard was different. Before he'd work on me, he insisted I have a complete physical workup—blood tests, heart tests, the whole thing.

Understand that at this point in my life, going to the doctor was not a regular part of my life. I saw a doctor when I was discharged from the Marines in 1968. The next time was in 1983, when my mother's doctor, Dr. Dalton, was about to retire and wanted to do me a favor by giving me a physical before he left his practice. He performed a little workup, and that's when I found out I had high blood pressure and began to get treatment for it.

So here it was twenty-one years past that, Dr. Howard in Birmingham wanted me to get a workup, and I didn't know what doctor to go to 'cause I didn't have one. I just wanted to go somewhere and get these tests knocked out so I could have my cosmetic procedure. My sister asked her bookkeeper for a recommendation for a doctor and, no, I don't know why she asked her bookkeeper for a recommendation for a doctor, but that's what she did. This gentleman said he'd see me, so that's where I made an appointment.

His nurse laid me down on the exam table, stuck ten little pads to my chest, and took an ECG, an electrocardiogram, which makes a recording of the electrical activity in your heart. It's a standard procedure, completely painless. You may have had one, yourself. But the next thing I knew, the people doing the test rushed out of the room and came back with the doctor. He said I needed another test right away. This time they put some gel on my chest and did an echocardiogram, which is basically an ultrasound like you do for a pregnant lady's belly except this one's for your heart. The bookkeeper's doctor did not like what he saw.

"You have a major issue here," he said. There were blockages in the vessels inside my heart, and he pointed them out on the monitor so I could see, too. He said this was so serious that he wanted to admit me to the hospital right then and there.

This was the last thing I expected. I was just doing what the cosmetic surgeon asked so I could get my nip and tuck. Now I was being told I have a life-and-death problem with my heart. "I don't want to frighten you," he said, "but Mr. Gregory, between here and the parking lot, you could drop dead."

Now this next part, some of you reading this are going to say I'm crazy, but a few of you are gonna say, "Yeah, that's probably what I'd do, too." So here it is. When a doctor says you might not make it to the parking lot, you're probably gonna do what he says. But I didn't. I suppose we all feel indestructible at times, and on this day I felt fine. There was another reason, too. This was at the end of April and in those days, May was one of my biggest months of the year. I booked all four weeks of May every year in Birmingham. I'd go down there, settle in, and get to do my shows in the same place, plus I would get to spend time with my good friend, Bruce Ayers. Plus, as I said, I felt fine.

With all that in my mind, I told him no. I made it out to the parking lot still upright, so I drove home. (When I told Bruce, he said I was crazy. I said, "But I gotta work to pay all those doctor bills!")

Still, you hear scary news like that, of course it sticks in your mind. A couple days later, I decided to go back so he could do another test, what's called an angiogram. This is where they put a tube into your groin, guide it up into your heart, and inject some dye. Then they take X-rays. Like the EKG, you can watch this one as it happens, and that's what I did.

The doctor proceeded to give me a personal lesson in cardiology by showing me exactly what was going on inside my very own heart at that moment. There are four main vessels where blood enters and leaves the heart. Two of mine were 95 percent blocked. A third was blocked to 80 percent. He showed me this. It couldn't have been any clearer, and that's what did it for me. I made the decision. I better go.

I thanked him for what he'd done but he wasn't accepting any of my praise for him. Instead, he told me how fortunate I was that I had seen Dr. Howard for my cosmetic surgery. He said that, as I knew, cosmetic surgery is mostly on the surface, not inside, so cosmetic surgeons rarely ask for heart tests. But Dr. Howard did, and it made all the difference.

"If you had gone under anesthesia," he said, "you would not have woken up. Dr. Howard saved your life."

***

You know me. Eventually, I made something funny out of it.

When I went into the hospital, I weighed 235 pounds. I spent a month in a medically induced coma and came out of the hospital at 190 pounds. Since then, my weight has fluctuated, like everyone's does, but when the scale says 190, I like to say I'm back down to my comatose weight.

People still ask me why I didn't see a doctor for all those years before. The answer's pretty funny: my heart doctor died of a heart attack. My dermatologist died of skin cancer. And my chiropractor had to quit because he had a bad back. So I did not have a lot of confidence in doctors overall.

That's one of those jokes where I stretch things a little, but not much. The part about the chiropractor, I made that up, but the rest is absolutely true. My first dermatologist really did die of skin cancer. As for my first heart doctor, that's true, too. Years before, I had been in Charlotte visiting with my old boss from sales days, Mike Wilson, a man you'll recall that I admire greatly. I wasn't feeling well and he insisted I go see his heart doctor. When Mike tells me something I take it seriously, so I made the appointment. This doctor did some tests and gave me the usual advice you get when there's nothing immediately wrong. He told me to lose weight, stop smoking, that sort of thing. But not long after, he dropped dead of a heart attack.

When a heart doctor drops dead of a heart attack, it does not inspire in me a great deal of confidence in the field as a whole.

One time I told this story on the radio, *The Big Show* with John Boy and Billy, and John Boy said flat out he didn't believe me. It was at that moment that the doctor's daughter called into the show to confirm it. Just goes to show you that truth is stranger than fiction.

When I'm on the radio, I'm always trying to steer the conversation to where the subject will naturally lend itself to something funny off the cuff. My good friends John Boy and Billy are especially talented at being funny in the moment, and that day everything went exactly right for all of us. After I had told this little story, John Boy asked me how my luck had gone with the proctologist.

"His name is Chad," I said. "But I'm done with Chad. I just don't believe that I need to see a proctologist every other weekend. Besides, I never get a bill!"

TESTING THE WATERS ON THE WEST COAST

There are several big comedy festivals each year. If you ever have the chance, you ought to go visit one. These are shows where dozens of comedians perform. There are huge audiences, of course, but the point of it is to get in front of TV and movie producers, plus people who book shows around the country. They're also an opportunity to get a little "buzz" going about how good you are at doing stand-up, to try to set yourself as the next big thing. One of the most important shows was the one HBO had sponsored for many years, the US Comedy Arts Festival, better known as the Aspen Comedy Festival, because that's where it was held for many years. In 2000, I was doing theaters in addition to comedy clubs. I figured this was a good opportunity to do the Aspen festival and see what might come of it.

Everybody was doing thirty to forty-five minutes, but I wanted an hour. It was like I had said years before to Jim McCawley at the Johnny Carson show: it takes me a while just to clear my throat. A half hour wasn't going to do it. My manager told this to the woman booking the show, a woman named Judi Brown, who in those days was a rising star as a producer, and who today is probably the most

160

powerful woman in comedy. Anyway, she was open to booking me for an hour, but she wanted to see my full-length show before she said yes. We flew her out to Charlotte to see my theater show at the Booth Playhouse. That was all it took. She booked me at the 2000 Aspen Comedy Festival.

It went very well—very, very well. At this point, it was suggested to me that with such a good reception, I ought to bring my show to Los Angeles for a longer run, a way to audition for the possibility of things like sitcoms, movies, TV appearances, and other kinds of work. That's what we did. We produced my show at the Hudson Theatre in Hollywood, California, with five weeks of shows Sunday through Thursday. You may notice that this is an odd schedule. The biggest shows of the week are on Friday and Saturday, yet those were days we let the house go dark. You have to remember why I was out there, which was to get exposure to people who might advance my career. They didn't need to see me on the weekend nights. Besides, I already had work booked for those days. On Friday morning I'd fly out from California to wherever I was working on the other side of the country, then fly back Sunday morning for the show that night at the Hudson.

But there was something else going on, something more important to me as a comedian and something more important to continue to build my career. I took this as an opportunity to weave together my routines into a true theater show. I had had a set built, something that looks like a front porch. You may have seen it yourself in person or on YouTube. Ultimately, I'd have it moved by truck from city to city. This was part of transforming what I'd done so far, working as a comedian with just a microphone in a club, into a performer using the stage itself to put on a theatrical performance with sets, lights, and "blocking," which just means planning how I move around on stage and how we use the space.

At the center of this was giving my show a dramatic arc, which really is the difference between doing routines in a nightclub and mounting a two-hour performance in a theater. I had always done my routines in a way that they build on one another, but now I was trying to make the whole thing into a single story with a beginning, a middle, and an end. I wanted it to add up to something that talked about my life and experiences. I also wanted to tell people what I think about various things—and make it even funnier than it was before. Five weeks at the Hudson let me get a lot of that figured out. I was very pleased with how this came out and eventually we filmed it as a television special.

During that time in LA, it was interesting to see how some in the crowds reacted. Many of the people in the audience were in the entertainment industry. They had been sent by their bosses to check me out, and they were not always happy about it. A lot of them had decided I was just a "Southern" comedian. You and I know that's not the case, but they didn't, so they had already made up their minds not to like me. You could tell from the way they sat, arms crossed, big frowns on their faces, basically saying *They told me I have to be here, so now I'm here. Show me what you got.*

I love that kind of a challenge. I would go up and do this two-hour show, much longer than the usual comedy show, and of course they'd find that although I'm a Southern man, what I talk about appeals to everyone, no matter where you live. That's what happened here, every night. By the end, these folks would be on their feet to applaud.

It was a valuable experience. Not only did it build the quality of my performance and my material, it also allowed me to transform what I had been doing into a next-level show for bigger venues and bigger audiences. Just as gratifying was to see that what I knew all along really was true: people are people wherever you go. If you tell 'em the truth and make 'em laugh while you're doing it, you'll do very well.

BIG IN A SMALL TOWN

O ne of the biggest changes in the comedy business has been the shift in some places from comedy clubs to theaters. These days, I work only a handful of comedy clubs, the ones in Nashville, Chattanooga, Birmingham, and Lexington. I appear in each of those cities twice a year. The rest is theater work.

I didn't just come up with the idea to work theaters and quit clubs. That never entered my mind. I moved to theaters when a club would go out of business or I no longer had a business connection to them. The first time this happened was when the comedy club in Raleigh, North Carolina, changed hands. I had been working there for twenty years and I needed a way to still see the people in the Raleigh area. Garner, Clayton, Selma, Holly Springs—I had never worked those smaller towns because I had been booked in Raleigh, less than fifty miles away. But with the change at the club, this amazing concentration of small towns became an opportunity. These places had theaters, and I booked them. Other cities followed the same pattern—Atlanta, for instance. As long as I was working at the Punchline there, I never worked any other place within a hundred miles. But when it changed hands, the many small towns nearby gave me a way to continue to make a living working that area.

As for the theaters themselves, most of them were built in the vaudeville era. After that, most of them closed. Pretty soon, many of them were abandoned, torn down, or converted into something else. Most of those still standing stood empty for decades. But in the past few years, more and more towns have refurbished these theaters. They're making them into performing arts locations—a place for local theater groups to perform, for showing classic movies, for community events and award ceremonies, and for entertainment from outside the community, which is where I come in.

These theaters usually seat between 250 and a thousand people, and it doesn't cost a lot to rent one. Bringing in a show was a new idea, a new way to make use of the space they'd worked so hard to revitalize. In some of these places, I was the first professional entertainer that had been on their stage since vaudeville. I'm enthusiastic about doing my show, and it turns out in these places that the people are just as excited as I am. You'll have the little old lady who sits in the box office three days a week in the afternoon selling tickets, plus you'll have tickets available at the laundromat and the dry cleaner and the grocery store, things like that. It becomes an event. At the height of this, I was working as many as fifty theaters a year. You'd be surprised how many of these theaters are out there, and there are dozens of towns that will support a night of entertainment a few times a year.

This is not a marketing strategy I came up with on my own. Actually, I stole it. Rather I "borrowed" from people who'd already been doing something like this for years, professional wrestlers.

Most people think of wrestling as something that got big when everybody got cable TV, but that's only partway true. It didn't get big. It got *bigger*—because it was already pretty big. Before cable, there were dozens of territories in the National Wrestling Alliance. (By the way, if you're wondering how I know all this about wrestling, it's because I love wrestling!) If you lived in Georgia, you kept up with Paul Jones and Georgia Championship Wrestling. In Tennessee, wrestling was run by Jerry Jarrett and his family along with Jerry's longtime business partner, the famous Jerry Lawler. In Oklahoma, it was "Cowboy" Bill Watts.

Here's how those wrestling promoters made their money. Consider a very big city like Atlanta. The promoters would put on a show in the 5500-seat Municipal Auditorium, which, in the 1960s and early 1970s, was the largest venue in Atlanta. But here's where it gets interesting: on Monday night they'd do the same show an hour up the road in the smaller town of Macon. The night after that, they'd go to the Bell Auditorium in Augusta. Then they'd work at the Township Auditorium just across the line in Columbia, South Carolina. This was the same show every time, the same big-name wrestlers, just in a venue less than half the size of the big venue in Atlanta.

Every promoter in every territory across America did it this way. They'd do a show in the big city, then the same show in smaller towns a half an hour to two hours away.

Why would they do that? Macon to Marietta is only an hour-and-a-half drive, and that's in traffic. Heck, Macon to Atlanta isn't much more than an hour. If someone wants to see wrestling, they'll make that drive to see it, right?

No, they won't. Here's why: it's about the people, not the distance. Once you stop thinking like the promoter and start thinking like the people in the audience, it makes perfect sense. People in those smaller towns live there for a reason. They had no interest in driving into downtown Atlanta on a weekend night, fighting all that traffic. For the man or woman who works Monday through Friday? To get in the car and drive an hour into the city, see a two-hour show, and drive back another hour? Most of them will say that's just too far to go.

But they'll for sure go to a show in their own town. The wrestling promoters figured that out and brought the show to them, and that's how "spot shows" were born.

That's what I did for comedy. I'm doing a spot show. Just like the wrestlers, I bring the show to them. What makes it possible is the existence of all these theaters. When it comes to very small towns, places with only a few thousand people, it's even more effective.

I thought this would work, and it has, and it continues to, but I was still surprised at how successful it turned out to be—even bigger than I expected. And I am continually humbled at how grateful people are to have my show in their own town. I can't tell you how many people would greet me with this: "We're so glad you came here! I thought I'd die before I saw you in person!" They'd say this even though I'd been performing no more than maybe ninety minutes away. They wouldn't drive into the nearest big city, but they'd sure come a few blocks to the theater in their own town. And it turns out you can always find a few hundred people who want to come out.

It's like that Jimmie Allen song, maybe you've heard it? It feels pretty good to be "Big in a Small Town."

Here's the Story: How to End Classroom Violence

"I'm the only person who can tell you the day classroom violence will end: the day the teacher shoots back."

We post a lot of my performances in short videos on YouTube and Facebook, and we always get a lot of likes and comments. But the most popular thing that we ever post is when I talk about classroom violence. People leave a comment because everybody has a strong opinion. As you know, I have a strong opinion, too. That's why I wrote the bit. And all I had to do was say what's on my mind.

When I tell you that my daddy wouldn't have stood for certain things in my house when I was a kid, that's the truth. (You can watch the video to hear exactly what daddy would have done.) My daddy was a man. He had a backbone like a steel rod. There wasn't "equity" in our family. He was in charge. And we stayed out of trouble 'cause there weren't excuses for getting into trouble. There were consequences.

Give the teachers guns! It's a joke—but think about it. If parents thought teachers were gonna shoot back, every parent in America would suddenly have time to make sure no kid is going to school with a gun. "You better not being going to school with a gun! That teacher'll kill your ass!"

NOTHING BETTER THAN HANGING OUT

There is one part of being a professional comedian that I do not believe the audience knows much about. For most of us, though, it's the best part, and there's nothing like it.

Some of the greatest times in my life have been onstage, but the very best times have been offstage, sitting in an IHOP at three in the morning trading war stories with other comedians. Many of those stories are what you're reading in this book. Didn't matter if you were a well-known headliner or an opener just starting out: sitting in a diner with the other comedians after the show is where you wanted to be. Still is.

We wanted something to eat after the show, and we had to leave the club 'cause it was closing. We didn't have day jobs, so we didn't have to get up in the morning. So we'd go somewhere and eat and just talk for hours about comedy and comedians and life on the road. It was either that or go back to the hotel all by yourself. So we would sit there swapping war stories. That's what we call 'em, war stories.

I've mentioned the wonderful Jeff Foxworthy already in this book. I want to mention him one more time. Before he was one of the most famous comedians in America, Jeff was like the rest of us, just getting started. He had quit his job working for IBM. (The story has always been that he quit his job before he had booked anything more than a couple weeks at the local club, the Atlanta Punchline. He was so thrilled to be doing comedy as a professional, he'd forgotten he needed regular income to pay his bills.) Anyway, he'd be down at the club and after the show was over, he and I and whoever else was working that night, plus whatever other comedians were at the club, we'd go across the street to the IHOP or the Waffle House and talk all night. We'd just talk comedy.

I remember another time at the Punchline. I was working with Jay Leno. I've already told you about a night in a diner with him and Steven Wright. This was before that and the other performer on the show this time was Paul Clay, a truly great monologist who would go on to write for *Designing Women*, *Evening Shade* with Burt Reynolds, and *The Arsenio Hall Show*, among many others. We ended up where comedians often went after a Punchline show, a place called the Beef Cellar, about a half mile away. It was open for food until 3 a.m. Paul and I were both from the Atlanta area and we were thrilled to hear stories from Jay and get his good advice.

Back in the Excelsior Mill days, at the very beginning of my time in comedy, I'd hang out after the show with my friend J. Anthony Brown. We'd go to the Huddle House, but we had no money. Of course you can't hang out in a restaurant without any money, especially if you're going to take up a table for three hours. You have to buy something, so we would split an order of raisin toast. A couple years ago, we were reminiscing about that.

"Gregory," he said to me, "don't you kinda wish it was forty-one years ago and we were broke? Splittin' that raisin toast?"

I said, "Heck no, man! Lemme tell you right now, no." He started laughing and so did I.

"You know what I mean," he said.

"Yeah, I do," I said.

"Things change," he said.

"Yeah, but it's bad and it's good," I said. "Nobody really wants to get old, but if you're not old, you're in the cemetery."

At that moment, the two of us were laughing, but we also had tears in our eyes. "We both came out all right, didn't we?" I said.

You don't get emotional when you meet someone at thirty-five and reminisce at forty-five. But when you come back to talk about the old times forty years later, it makes you think. It's happy and sad at the same time, know what I mean? Those road stories are the stories of our lives.

***

The biggest "hang out" I was ever a part of didn't happen in a diner. Every year from 1988 to 2007, I had a giant Christmas party at my house. I'd even do the cooking.

Since comedians work on the weekend, the party was always on a Monday in early December. Everybody I know in comedy would come out: professionals, local guys, comedians just passing through, comedians' wives, club owners, fellas who had just heard it was happening, anybody else that was a part of the comedy business. I'd have a hundred or so people every year. And late into the night, about the same time as when a show would be over in a nightclub, we'd settle in and start telling stories.

You know me, I'm always happy to tell my stories, too. Some of the comedians would call it "holding court." Not me. I never call it that. Sounds arrogant. But we would share those war stories, the same ones we'd all been swapping over the table in late-night diners, the Waffle House, the IHOP, and everywhere else.

The thing is, they didn't want to hear the latest things that had happened to me. They wanted to hear the old stories again, the ones we'd all shared together in those late-night sessions. If I wasn't telling the story they wanted to hear, they'd trick me into it. They'd start telling it themselves until finally I'd break in. "No, no, no, that's not how it happened"—and I'd give 'em the story they remembered. Once we'd get past three or four in the morning, the "civilians"—the people who weren't comedians—would hang it up and go back home or to the hotel or the condo or wherever. The rest of us? Lots of those Christmas party nights, we'd keep going until the sun came up. A bunch of comedians doing the thing we love more than anything, telling war stories. Nothing like it.

COPS AND CARS

As I've said, every year I have a different name for my tour. One year, I had added a bit to my routine about tornadoes. I'd mention that when a tornado tears through a trailer park, the guy they interview always has a tattoo and a tire gauge. The tattoo is usually something like "Mom"—and it's misspelled. And he's carrying around a tire gauge in case his living room doesn't seem level. This line would bring down the house, so I decided I'd sell real tire gauges with the tour name printed on them.

Keep in mind this was long before the internet so you couldn't just type into Amazon, "Sell me some tire gauges by the gross." You'd have to ask around. I was in Texas, traveling with the very funny, very clean comedian Steve Mingolla. He was opening the shows for me, so we were driving from place to place together. Anyway, I pulled off at a little convenience store, not one of the modern big ones with a name brand, one of the little local ones. Behind the counter was a pegboard, where you hang hooks so you can display things. They had all the usual things you'd expect: Rolaids, Stanback powder (you might have to look that up, it's an old one), and a few other things including tire gauges.

I figured the young man behind the counter might be able to help me. Thing is, I didn't phrase my question quite right. I was wondering why people buy a tire gauge, what they say to this guy. This sounds like a weird question, but in those days, it was a reasonable thing to ask because this was before you had a light on your dashboard for low tire pressure. Anyway, I wanted him to tell me what reason people give him, like did they hear a funny sound, or was the car pulling a little, things like that. So what I asked him was, "What do you sell those tire gauges for?"

"To see how much air's in the tire," he said.

I chuckled and said, "No, I mean how much?"

"Well, sir," he said, "most tires take about thirty-two pounds."

At that point, I gave up. Steve and I just got back in the car and left.

***

Here's one more car story. One night, I was staying at a hotel in Brentwood, Tennessee, when the phone in my room rang. "Mr. Gregory, there is a police officer down here in the lobby and he would like to speak with you."

I went down there and the officer explained the situation. "Somebody has reported that your car is parked in a handicapped spot," he said.

"Yes, it is," I said.

"Well, sir, your permit isn't hanging from the mirror."

"Yep," I said. "I laid it on the dashboard. The plastic hook is cracked. How come you're out here in the middle of the night checking handicapped spots, anyway?"

"Mr. Gregory, somebody saw your car and reported that they didn't see the permit."

"Are you kidding? That's all it takes to get a policeman out here?"

"I understand, sir, but could you go ahead and put it on the mirror anyway? So when some crackpot"—that was his word, not mine—"drives in, he'll see it?" Now came the question which, it turns out, he had come to ask me in the first place. "Mr. Gregory, what do you have in the trunk of that car?"

"That's none of your business," I said.

"We might need to take a look in your trunk."

"Not without a warrant, you're not."

"I can make a call to the K-9 people. You want that?"

"I don't mind. I love dogs."

I was standing in the parking lot of a hotel next to the interstate in Brentwood, Tennessee. It was three in the morning and a cop was threatening to call backup and the K-9 unit to go through the trunk of my car over a crack in handicapped parking permit. About this time, another officer pulled up—backup! The first officer caught him up. "We have a fellow here who doesn't want me to see what's in the trunk of his car," he said.

"I didn't say that," I said. "I told him he could see inside there with a warrant."

Now the second cop spoke up. "We can't get a warrant. We have no probable cause." Then he started to smile, but I could tell he was trying not to. "Mr. Gregory, do you mean to tell me that if we were to open the trunk of your car, we would not find any DVDs and CDs in there?"

"Officer, all that stuff is down at the comedy club where I'm working."

"Mr. Gregory, do you mean we have come all the way out here and we can't get one of your comedy CDs?"

They started to laugh. Suddenly I got it, and I started laughing too. "Tell you what, gentlemen. You give me your names and addresses and I'll send you some stuff. How about that?"

And for the rest of my time at that Brentwood hotel, I did not get any more calls about my parking permit.

***

One last car story to wrap it up. One time I was traveling from Nashville to do a show in Branson, Missouri. That is a long drive, about five hundred miles in more than seven hours. Once you get west of the Illinois line into Missouri, that part of the state is almost entirely corn fields and empty spaces. I was riding that stretch with Lenny, who came along for the show, when a state trooper appeared out of nowhere, lights blazing. One more time, I was not happy to be bothered when I wasn't doing anything wrong. (You know I wasn't speeding, and you know why: that threat to tell my daddy back when I was sixteen took care of that.) The officer came up to the window and did the usual business, then asked me to come back with him to his car. I sat back there with him for a long time. Meanwhile, as the minutes went on, Lenny was getting more and more worried about what in the world was going on.

Twenty minutes later, I came back to the car, and my manager was beside himself. He could not imagine what was going on back there that wasn't going to end in trouble for both of us. "Everything okay? We getting hauled in? What's wrong?"

He was worked up, but I was laughing. "I don't think we're gonna get too many years in prison for this one," I said. Turns out the trooper had run my tags and realized who I was. He was a big fan and wanted to meet me, and maybe get a DVD or a CD. I had sat back there and visited with him for a while just to enjoy the break from driving—plus to prank Lenny and give him a little something to worry about.

Once in a while, you need to remind your manager who's in charge, don't you think?

This trip to Branson was to work with Terry Fator, a comedian who does ventriloquism, or what they call in the entertainment business a "vent act." He's a funny guy, and he was a successful headliner many years when we were working together, even before he won *America's Got Talent.*

When my last show of the week is over, it doesn't matter where I'm headed next, I wanna get there as quick as I can even if it's to go back home. Doesn't matter how late it is or how long the drive, I hit the road. I'm used to those late-night drives but not everybody else is, including my manager. We left in the middle of a storm, headed through the Ozark Mountains. Lenny drove and I went to sleep. I can sleep through anything, and I was out cold inside of a minute.

The rain was beating down on the metal roof of this Cadillac to the point where you couldn't hear yourself think. I was sleeping through it like it was nothing. Then about a hundred yards ahead, lightning struck. It lit up everything all around, like day for night, and it sounded like an explosion. I sat up for just a second, whipped my head around, and I said, "What was that?" The next second I was right back asleep. But of course now Lenny was wide awake, white-knuckling it through this storm in the mountains where he could barely see out the windshield.

I can sleep in a car, anytime, anyplace, any weather. I've long said that I need to find me somebody who can build me a bed that looks like the front seat of a Cadillac.

IT'S NOT ENOUGH TO BE FUNNY

The other day I was figuring up how many shows I've done in my career. For most of the time since the 1980s I worked about forty-eight weeks a year, nine shows a week. That's about 450 shows a year. Recently I've worked theaters more often than clubs, so there were years I did maybe 150 shows a year and, later, about seventy shows a year. So I'll say I've done at least ten thousand shows, probably more.

As for where I've been, I've performed in thirty-three states. I've also performed in the Middle East, as you know, parts of Europe, and I've made several visits to Canada, from Saskatoon to Nova Scotia, and to beautiful Banff Springs, which is a part of a breathtaking Canadian national park. I was in Canada for corporate gigs, meaning that I was hired as the entertainment for an event that a company was putting on. That's worth talking about here because comedians are always hoping for a corporate gig. The obvious attraction is the money. These shows tend to pay very well, usually better than club work and even some theater gigs. They are preferable to a theater show because you or the people who work for you don't have to work out transporting a set to the venue. They are preferable to a club gig because the travel is usually taken care of: they get you there, drive you around, put you up for the night, then send you home. All you have to do is perform.

What's less known is they can also be the most difficult shows to do. You're brought in not because you've sold tickets to your fans. You're there because the person in charge of booking it likes you. Doesn't matter if anybody else thinks your funny or has even heard of you. When I did my show in Saskatoon, about half the audience was American and might know who I am, but the other half was Canadian and they didn't know me from Adam. Fortunately, all it takes to appreciate what I do is to have an appreciation for common sense. Getting it does not depend on living in one place or another.

The potential problem is that the audience didn't come out to hear comedy. They're there because this is a banquet or an awards ceremony. They may not even know there's going to be a comedy show. Sometimes they don't have a choice—the boss told them they had to be there. Then there's the fact that if it's a weeknight, they've already been working all day, and they may want to go home and relax a lot more than they want to see you. They may even leave in the middle of it!

These shows are often a test of just how strong a comedian you are, how professional you are in the sense that you can handle any situation. It takes experience. It also takes a little modesty, because you can't force people to laugh no matter how funny you are. You have to have the skill to bring them along.

Lemme tell you a story I was told about a corporate gig from back in the '80s featuring Jerry Seinfeld and The Amazing Jonathan. In those days, these two acts were at about the same level in terms of drawing power. This was before Jerry had his TV show. He was a skilled monologist but he was still a road warrior, and he made his living in theaters and nightclubs. The Amazing Jonathan, who passed away rather young in 2022, was a different kind of act. He was a whirlwind. He really was. He did magic, stunts, and comedy, generally making a mess of the stage along the way.

On this night, Jonathan and Jerry were both doing forty-five minutes and Jonathan went up first. He "killed," as we say. He sucked the air out of the room. He exhausted the audience, and Jerry Seinfeld had to follow that!

The corporate host came up in between, spoke for a couple minutes, then introduced Seinfeld. This is where it takes a pro. There was no following Jonathan. No way could a thoughtful monologist follow a guy who just drank a bottle of Windex and sawed through his arm with a kitchen knife. Jerry knew that for his first fifteen or twenty minutes, he was gonna eat it, so he accepted it. But he knew how to get through that. For the first third of his show, he held back his "A" stuff. He knew that it wouldn't matter how strong it was, the audience wasn't ready. He had to "waste" some time until they had calmed down and gotten used to this quieter show at a slower pace. This allowed him to not waste his best material but save it for the back half, when they'd eat it up.

That's just what he did. Forty-five minutes later, they gave him a standing ovation.

Being a comedian isn't just about being funny. It's about being comfortable in your own skin. It's about putting your experience with an audience to work when it's do-or-die time. Even after years of shows, not all comedians have that kind of skill. But when you see it, it's amazing.

Here's the Story: Funeral Home Gossip

"She didn't bake that ham. It had pineapple rings and cherries on it. That's a Winn-Dixie ham right there!"

People like to hear this story because everybody knows this is exactly what happens.

When I was a kid and somebody passed away, it'd take three days to have the funeral. Everybody'd show up with a covered dish. It always intrigued me that people would sit around talking more about the food and who brought what than about the guy who died. "I see Elizabeth brought that macaroni salad. I knew she'd do this. I guarantee if it'd been somebody on her side of the family, she'da brought some kind of meat."

We had a neighbor, Mr. Tate. He had a one-chair barber shop in downtown Lithonia. No matter who died in our town, Mrs. Tate would always be there. I remember she'd always complain about whoever brought the sweet potato pie. "It's got nutmeg in it. I can't eat nutmeg. I don't know why people can't make a sweet potato pie without nutmeg in it." That was her concern instead of the poor guy who died. It's a little cold to say, but me and my brother grew up so poor, sometimes we'd sorta be glad somebody had died so we could eat a good meal.

I told this story on an episode of Country's Family Reunion sitting right next to Charlie Pride. I thought he was gonna die laughing at it!

A LIST OF DON'TS

When a young comedian asks me for advice, it's rarely about how to improve his act. More often, it's about whether I can introduce him to a club owner or put in a good word for him somewhere. I'm happy to do that, but that's not what they need most.

As I say to any comedian who will listen, what they need to keep in mind at all times is that this is a business, and if they treat it that way, they're far more likely to succeed. Treat it like a vocation, not a vacation. Here are few of my own rules for what not to do:

Don't be rude to the club owner. Be respectful to the person who hires you, who employs you, and who pays you. Always.

Don't burn bridges. When you have a disagreement, be civil. Work it out calmly. Preserve the relationship.

Don't sleep with the waitresses.

Don't just be on time. Be early. Don't make it so the people who rely on you have to worry about where you are.

Don't do more time than you're supposed to. The people who work there want to go home when the show is scheduled to be over. That's more important than you having fun on stage.

Don't do less time than you're supposed to, either. The time you're on stage is when the club makes money selling food and drink. Don't cut into that. The audience expects to be entertained for the full time they paid for. Give it to them. The staff needs time to get out the checks, too. If you leave the stage early, the servers have to get people to settle up while they're trying to leave, and that's a mess.

Don't expect to make it as a professional if you're not in 100 percent. Where I live, near Atlanta, there are dozens of people who are comedians. Some of them are even funny. But if I call one of them today and say I'm going to be in Lexington, Kentucky, next week for four days and I need an opening act, they'll say they'd love to but they can't get off their "real" jobs. Those aren't professional comedians. There's not much of a future for a comedian who can only work on his own schedule. It's a commitment and a sacrifice. That's why there are more brain surgeons than there are full-time professional comedians.

I've mentioned my friend Jeff Gilstrap from Lexington. He used to say that you can tell right away which comedians are going to be successful, because when the show is over, you look around and you can't find them. Performers who are serious about their careers won't be hanging around the bar after the show. They know better than to make themselves seem like nothing special to the audience. That's another reason we all end up at Waffle House or some all-night diner. It's not that I believe comedians have to live like monks. What I'm saying is that you have to protect your reputation and your future, and you have to conduct yourself professionally in front of other people. If you're going to let your hair down, do it where it's safe to let go.

It's better for a club owner and the staff to know you by what you do on stage than by who you are offstage, and that's true even if you are well behaved everywhere they see you. I want that club owner to say, "When James is here, I sell more food and drinks, I'm busy the whole time, people give compliments more often about my club, and we sell out right away. I love it when James comes to town." It doesn't need to go any further than that.

EARNING MY WAY TO HEADLINER

One part of the business I haven't talked much about is how I earned my way to headliner. You don't get "invited" to move up. It's not like getting asked to a Christmas party. You move up only when you earn it, and that's on you. There's no other way.

For years, comedy shows have consisted of an emcee or "opener," who does ten or fifteen minutes including announcements, a feature or "middle," who does twenty minutes to a half hour, and a headliner or "closer," who does forty-five minutes to an hour. Like everybody else, I started as an opener. There are no exceptions. (Actually, there is one exception, the only one I know of. I could have started as feature, but you'll remember that I lost a coin toss to J. Anthony Brown. So he's the exception!)

How do you get to be an opener? Jay Leno, Jerry Seinfeld, Eddie Murphy, Bill Burr. Ask 'em how they got started and they'll all give the same answer: open mic night. You can't go get a diploma in comedy. You have to prove you're funny in front of the people. To earn your way onto the stage, you'll work amateur nights and open mic shows for free, and you'll do it for a long, long time.

You may get a lot of laughs your first time up, but nobody is born with the talent to do stand-up comedy professionally. You have to learn, and there's a lot to learn. For instance, you have to learn to perform successfully for every kind of audience: rowdy audiences, quiet audiences, tiny audiences, audiences already worn out from what came before. This comes only from experience, and lots of it—daily experience over the long haul. You can't just go up once or twice a week. The only way to get good at this is to do it night after night, sometimes several shows a night, for year after year. No one has ever succeeded any other way. Anyone who tells you otherwise is pulling your leg.

How do you earn your way up from emcee to feature to headliner? It's like the old joke about two fellas running away from a bear. The first guy says to the other, "I sure hope I can outrun that bear." Then the other guy says, "I don't have to outrun the bear. I just have to outrun you." The way you move up is to be better than the guy who has to go on after you. An opener has to outshine the feature. The feature has to smoke the headliner. As I always say, you can't get there on a dream. You need a goal, and that goal takes a plan.

Here's how my plan worked. A lot of comedians use the first few shows of the week to experiment with material or try to impress the club owner or the staff, or just to amuse themselves. Not me. A paying show is no place for that. I was there to move up. Once I had twenty-five minutes of material the headliner hated, I wouldn't change a word. Why would the headliner hate my act? Because he knew that if he couldn't follow me, I could get booked into his slot. Worst case for him, they might switch us out in the middle of the week and make me the headliner for the weekend shows.

The Punchline in Columbia, South Carolina, was owned by Robo Walker. The guys in Atlanta, Ron DiNunzio and Dave Montesano, booked the talent for all the Punchlines, including the one Robo owned. I had been the feature act for Robo several times. For a few of those, the headliners had trouble following me. This was one of those weeks, so Robo changed the order. Now I would be the closer and the headliner would be the feature. It made the other comedian so angry he tried to start a fistfight with me.

"I work for the same guy you do," I said. "I'm just doing what he told me to do."

"I'm gonna kick your ass!"

"You don't wanna do that," I said. He wasn't gonna kick anybody's ass. He was just mad that he got bumped down, and he knew how this works. If you *can't* follow the feature, you don't *want* to follow the feature. You're the one who'll look bad, not the middle. This was humiliating for him, but Robo saved him considerable embarrassment. Besides, nobody knew about the switch but us.

At the end of the week, Robo sat down to write me my paycheck. While he was doing that, he called Ron DiNunzio in Atlanta, and he signaled to me to not say a word. I couldn't hear Ron's end of the conversation, but I heard every word from Robo.

"Ron," he said, "I'm writing James Gregory's final paycheck. I don't want him back here unless he's the headliner." There was a pause while Ron answered him, and then Robo said, "I know you book the acts, but I own this place. I'm not saying you have to book him as a headliner everywhere, I'm saying I don't want him back here unless he's the headliner."

The next week I was in Atlanta, hanging out at the Punchline when Ron came up to me. "They tell me you're a headliner," he said.

I smiled. "I guess we'll see what happens."

From then on, I was a headliner at all the Punchlines—except Atlanta. It's hard to make it in your hometown.

A few things can help you move up. Having a presence on TV always helps—of course, I've told you why I didn't have much of that and why it didn't stop me. More important than anything is the fact that comedy is a business. You put the strongest performer on top because he's worked his way up there. No club owner has ever said, "You've been a feature act long enough. It's time for that promotion." You have to earn your way to it, and I did.

WHAT I DO WHEN I'M NOT DOING COMEDY

I like to watch comedy, but probably not as much as you think. I'll watch somebody's show in little segments, never the whole routine, because I have this fear that I might subconsciously absorb something they say that may pop out later. I'll catch them on YouTube. I especially like seeing a comedian be interviewed, doing ad lib material, and answering questions. I enjoy that more than watching forty-five minutes of stand-up.

As for who I like, I've always liked Dave Chappelle. I love him now more than ever because the "woke" community hates him. Same with Bill Burr. I'm a big fan of his. Never met him, but he's great. Notice I'm saying only that I like these folks. I'm not saying they're the best. You can't say one is so much better than another because different people like different things.

***

I love to play the lottery. Since back in the 1990s, even the 1980s, I've played the lottery. I'd spend about one hundred dollars a week on it, though in the past few years I've cut back to fifty dollars a

190

week. And since I travel all over the country, I know the details for the games in all the states I visit—what day the drawings are on, how much the jackpot is, that sort of thing. Some lotteries involve several states. There's a Powerball drawing three days a week: Monday, Wednesday, and Saturday. Mega Millions is on Tuesday and Friday. This is the kind of information that is interesting to me.

I have friends who buy lottery tickets only when it gets up to a certain amount. It drives me crazy. The ticket is only two dollars. When the jackpot is $40 million, somehow that's not enough for them. But when it gets up around $150 million, they're interested. I'm making a joke about it here, but it's a joke I didn't have to write! All I'm doing is telling you what they said. Let me tell you something: whatever the jackpot is, it's more than I have now. Heck, Mega Millions starts at $20 million. That's for sure more than I have. I think I'll risk two dollars.

You might say I'm obsessed with entering the lottery, but I'm not obsessed with finding out if I won. If somebody wins the jackpot, they'll announce it. If I don't hear my name, I'll get around later to looking into it. Maybe I won second place! You have six months to check your tickets. If it's not the jackpot, I can wait six months.

You're probably wondering: in all these years of playing the lottery, what's the most I ever won? Twenty bucks.

One more thing: I don't buy my tickets online. I go into the convenience store or the supermarket and get them there. I don't do anything online. I don't bank online. I go in the front door of the bank. I don't look at my bank statements online. I get 'em in the mail. I don't pay bills online, either. If I owe you money, I'll write you a check and drop it in the mail. And I don't hire anybody to write those checks for me. I write my own checks.

I like what I can hold in my hand. Feels a lot more certain that way.

***

I've told you that I like nice things. One of those is a Cadillac.

When I was a young man in the 1960s and 1970s, a Cadillac was the nicest car you could buy. Driving a Cadillac meant you had arrived. I bought my first one when I was in the sales business. Of course, at that time I was flush. After I switched to comedy, it was many years before I could even think about being able to afford another one. At the same time, I have to tell you that these cars I buy are never as expensive as they could be because I haven't bought a new car in thirty years. I let somebody else buy the new ones, drive off that high price for a year or two, then I buy mine used.

When I started to travel doing comedy and could finally afford to buy something instead of borrowing my dad's truck, I ended up with a 1978 Coupe DeVille. I knew a comedian named Russ Fisher who was about to trade up for a 1985 Eldorado, but instead of trading it, he sold it to me and, very kindly, he let me pay him when I could. So I hit the road in a Cadillac Coupe DeVille. That model would be my car of choice for many years—always used, of course. I'd buy one and drive it for a long time, then I'd buy another, and another, and another.

Also, as I've said, I wanted my mother and father to have what they would like, too, so I always bought them cars as well, sometimes handing off to them the Cadillacs I took on the road. One time, I had a Coupe DeVille that I was ready to get rid of. The thing is, my parents didn't need to replace their car at the time, but they had friends who needed a car and couldn't afford one. So we gave that Coupe DeVille to them instead. That should have been the end of the story except for this. I was sitting at the kitchen table with my mother and father when my mother said that the neighbor lady was having a bit of a problem. A Coupe DeVille is not a sedan with four doors, it's a two-door car. Mom said the neighbor lady didn't like the car so much because it was hard to get kids and grandkids in and out of the back seat.

My dad said, "Dammit, it's a free Cadillac! Who cares if it's hard to get your kids in the back seat?" Mom had to admit, he had a good point.

So I'm a Cadillac person, but my dad was always a Ford man. When I was in the sales business, I bought my dad a brand-new 1973 Ford pickup. That was a proud moment for me. Years later, when I had money again, I kept up the tradition of giving him a Ford. One time, though, I broke that tradition and gave him a Cadillac. A couple years later, their fiftieth anniversary was approaching. I wanted to buy my dad something special. Again, I was sitting at the kitchen table across from mom and I told her I figured I would buy Dad a new Ford.

"I'm not sure you ought to," she said. "He doesn't like to talk about this, but your dad really likes that Cadillac." I wanted to buy him what he wanted so I asked him myself.

"Son, you know me. I'm a Ford guy. But the last couple of years all of my friends and the neighbors have seen me in that Cadillac you bought me."

"That's a good thing," I said.

"Yes, it is," he said. "Thing is, if I suddenly show up in a Ford, they might think you're not doing well!"

***

Every year or so, I call my niece or a friend of mine to make a socks-and-underwear run to Goodwill—I accumulate socks and underwear I never even take out of the package. That's just one of the things in my life that has changed considerably from where I began. When I was a boy, we were so poor that when our clothes got worn out, my mother would patch them with a flour sack. It's what poor people did back then. You'd buy flour in a cloth sack that held twenty-five pounds. After you'd used up the flour, you'd save the sack. You could make a blouse out of it, or a dress, or you could use it to patch up clothes. My mother did all that. Sometimes she wasn't picky about where she cut a piece out of the sack to use as a patch. As a result, sometimes she'd cut a pink flower out of the flour-company logo and patch my underwear with it. The other kids would tease me about it when we got dressed for gym class.

I think that's why I buy more socks and underwear than I'll ever need: I never want to run out. I'm afraid I'll have to wear raggedy underwear!

At this point, I'm the same about shirts and shoes. It's not that I'm a fashion plate. I dress for comfort, not for style, but I don't want to run out! I buy shirts all the time, more than I can ever wear, then hang 'em in the closet. I fill it up every few years, then I call my nieces or nephews to take some to Goodwill. Last time they were here, they took a few yards of hang-up dress shirts. When I was a kid and the soles would come loose from our shoes, my mother would put a big rubber band around the shoe. It didn't fix the sole, but it kept it from flopping around. Maybe I shouldn't complain, though. I remember one time my mother bought me brand-new clothes. It was a lavender shirt and a yellow pair of pants.

I liked the flour sack better.

RETIREMENT?

I have no plans to retire.

As long as people keep coming out to see me perform, why in the world would I want to stop?

In this business, and at this point in my life, I can choose the number of weeks I want to work. I don't have to get somebody's permission to work, or to take a day off. All I have to do is go to a place where they want to see James Gregory, then get on that stage and deliver what people came to see. I love doing it and I'm gonna keep at it.

If I had chosen another occupation, I would have had to retire a long time ago. I know that 'cause that's what happened with my family and with the people I grew up around. I come from a background of people who do manual labor for a living, what you call blue-collar workers, people who work with their backs and their hands. Carpenters. Truck drivers. That sort of thing. And that's a hard row to hoe. Let' s say you're a roofer. Part of your job is putting a hundred pounds of roofing tiles over your shoulder and carrying them up a ladder in the hot sun. At this point, if I was a roofer, I'd have had to retire a long time ago. You get much up past sixty, you're not going to be a roofer. In fact, you're not going to be doing much of any kind of manual labor. Drive past a construction site and see how many guys that age are out there working.

In some cases, you don't have a choice. After a certain point, for instance, a long-haul truck driver can't get a license anymore, not because of their age but because they can't pass the vision test or the physical examination. In those jobs, you come to a point where you have to retire—and you have to do it whether or not you have money in the bank. So I'm grateful that I could retire if I wanted to, even though I don't want to. I'm grateful that I do not want to retire. And I'm grateful that I'll never have to.

I think that doing comedy may make you live longer, anyway. Have you noticed that in the entertainment business, it's the comedians who live the longest? Bob Hope lived to be a hundred years old. So did George Burns. Betty White was three weeks shy of one hundred. Don Rickles was ninety. Jackie Mason was ninety-three. Henny Youngman was just shy of ninety-two. Milton Berle was ninety-three. Shelley Berman made it to ninety-two. Bob Newhart, Mel Brooks, and Dick Van Dyke are all in their nineties and still performing as I'm sitting here writing this in 2024. Maybe there's something to that old saying about laughter being the best medicine.

A lot of people aren't very good at retirement. You and I both have known people who retire, and it's fine for the first six months. After that, though, they don't seem quite as happy as they thought they would be. You can only watch television or read a book so much. Then you have those people who say, "I'm gonna spend more time with my grandkids."

I wanna say to them, "How much more time do you think they want to spend with you?" You don't have to quit your job to spend more time with people you love. I'm pretty sure my nieces and nephews don't want me over at their house every day from now on. Don't wear out your welcome!

Even if you retire, you still have to have a reason to get up in the morning. One time I heard a guy say, "When I retire, the first thing I'm gonna do is take care of my own yard."

I said, "Excuse me?"

"Oh, yeah!" he said. He was excited about it.

"Lemme see if I got this right," I said. "I want to keep working to pay somebody to keep me *out* of that yard. But you want to retire so you don't have to pay the landscaper. We are direct opposites."

For a lot of people, it's not retirement they really want. They just want to work a little less.

I was talking to someone about a comedian we both knew who was talking about retiring. I wasn't so sure he'd go through with it. "Let's say the power company wants him to do a one hour show at their annual convention for $6,000," I said. "Do you think he'd want to do that?"

"Oh, yeah. He'd do that."

"Then he's not retired," I said. "He's just being pickier about when he works."

I *could* quit. After spending all these years on the road, and with all of you being so supportive of what I do, I could retire— but I don't want to, not at all.

I'm just being honest with you.

When you see me on stage these days, it's because I want to be there and you want me to be there. Simple as that. I am fortunate to be in that position. I'm also fortunate that I'm not one of those comedians who has to be on stage in order to feel like I'm "alive." A lot of performers, I'd say most of them, tell me that they feel empty inside if they're not on stage, not getting that applause. My perspective is different. I love being on stage, but could I get by without it? Of course I could. I would prefer to be on stage, but I wouldn't be suicidal if I couldn't get on stage again. These days, and it's been this way for many years, I don't have to go up. I'm there because I want to go up—and because people come out to see me.

People say so many kind things about me and about my comedy. I appreciate it, I really do. But I have to tell you that it works both ways. In return for the laughter I got to give to you, you've given me even more: a wonderful life, wonderful experiences, wonderful friends, and nearly fifty years doing what I love, living the life of a professional comedian.

I will always be grateful, always.

THE END (FOR NOW...)

A FEW WORDS FROM ALL Y'ALL

I decided the best way to finish this book was for me to hush up and give all y'all the last word. Here are some of the comments that have come in over the years from all kinds of people from all around the world with one thing in common: they love to laugh, just like me. Thanks for helping me wrap up my book on a high note!

Sincerely, James Gregory

***

"Your comedy is real. No fluff. No excuses. No tiptoeing around whatever subject you're addressing. You say what many of us think but don't have the platform to say or are just plain too afraid to say. Your comedy teaches us to laugh at ourselves, our upbringing, and those in our lives who just really worked at and deserve to be the object of our humor. I'm sure you've seen people who try not to laugh because they are worried about what someone else may think. Well, your comedy breaks these type barriers and causes people to absolutely 'burst' or as you would say, 'bust' out in laughter—that 'can't help it' kind of laughter; that 'I should have worn a Depends' kind of laughter. What a legacy to be able to say that you left everyone a *real laugh!* There is nothing more valuable than a laugh! Thank you for giving me so many!"

—Lee Barnes, Opp, Alabama

"A way to relate all my childhood growing up put into words."

—Brenda Naftel, Foley, Alabama

"Always…made me laugh on some of my worst days. It never grows old. Pure, clean enjoyment. You are truly the Funniest Man in America. The best! God bless you. Keep on doing what you do: you are the best at making people laugh."

—David Watkins, Marble, North Carolina

"James Gregory is an A-list elite comic. Three generations of my family have learned and laughed from him for hours upon end. He absolutely nails his craft!"

—Michael Fagan, Columbia, Tennessee

"Just when I thought wokeness had killed comedy, I discovered James Gregory and saw comedy was indeed still alive and well. James is a funny storyteller who doesn't have to rely on the tired old crutch of using raunchiness to get laughs."

—Toby Ellington, Fitzgerald, Georgia

"A good laugh and a heap of common sense."

—Kregg W. Eason, Mulberry, Florida

"As a disk jockey at WMPI-FM in Scottsburg, Indiana, we got a lot of promotional CDs, almost all of them musical, but one day we were sent two copies of *It Could Be a Law, I Don't Know.* I saw the name James Gregory and I thought, well that's the guy on *Barney Miller*, ain't it? But it didn't look like him on the cover, so I put it in the player to give it a listen. The emcee said this guy was the 'funniest man in America.' That guy was right. Thank God I wasn't driving because I believe I would've hit two trees and a guard rail laughing at that album…and it would have been worth it. Like I said, the station got two copies. One is still there (and so am I, by the way). The other one… well…is now in a private collection…"

—Todd Richmond, New Albany, Indiana

"Commonsense jokes and heaps of laughter!"

—Wayne, New Zealand

"First time I saw one of your shows was seven years after my grandmother died and I was working for the Dothan, Alabama, opera house. One of your bits reminded me of her so much. I laughed so hard I cried. By the time I regained myself, I didn't know if I was crying because of memories you brought back to the surface or because it was really that hilarious. I will forever be grateful to you for that and it was truly one of the best shows I ever worked with there. Thank you, Mr. James Gregory."

—Amy Franklin, Dothan, Alabama

"I'm not an American, though I wanted to be before wokeness started. I'm a Filipino living in New Zealand. I truly enjoy the way you unpack the good old traditional American culture and values in a funny, sometimes hilarious way, but strike deep into the hearts of commonsense people. They may laugh, but then they think, *Why did we just sit idly by and let these stupid things that broke down our family, community, country, and future, happen?* I pray there's time to go back, clean up, and become what it used to be. Bless you, Sir."

—A Fan, New Zealand

"Hearing your stories always sends me back in time to my aunts and my mom. Every story was a story of someone I once knew!"

—Cathy DiSante, Lafayette, Louisiana

"Being real is what I like and you make me laugh while being real! Thank you so much!"

—David Jones, Elmendorf, Texas

"I discovered you only about two years ago and live in the UK. What I like so much about your comedy is that it is mostly about old-fashioned morals and respect for each other and the fact we can have a laugh about it. Absolutely brilliant!"

—Steven Brown, Kent, England

"I am a professional clown that grew up in the country. I found you on the internet. In a time of political correctness, your clean comedic stories and views are spot-on with timing and delivery. Your stories bring back memories of back in the day. I would almost swear that you had to have been in my neighborhood! (Please come to Sarasota, Florida, Circus Capital of the World, because even clowns need to laugh.)"

—A Fan, Sarasota, Florida

"Honestly, your comedy sparked my interest in the whole form of communication. I was about twelve or thirteen when I went to one of your shows in Amarillo, Texas. I was determined not to laugh. I failed. In fact, I failed so miserably that I had several belly laughs. Through the years I have followed your career, been to a few shows, watched your clips on social media. Ten years ago, I started doing comedy as a pastime for rotary clubs, churches, and other non-profits. Because of this my son wanted to do stand-up for his fourth-grade talent show, and that began his love of the stage and medium as well. Your comedy began a multigenerational love for making people laugh! I don't know about being included in your book, but if I ever write one, you'll be included in mine. You have to give credit where it's due. Thanks for the laughs. Your comedy has helped shape me both as a comedian and a person, and I passed it on to the next generation."

—Kurt Jones, Canyon, Texas

"You have been the light in the dark and a port in the storm. That is what your comedy is for me."

—Daniel Cayea, Lyon Mountain, New York

"When I listen to you, I forget about my worries for even just a while. I can laugh until my cheeks and stomach hurt. It's an escape. Being a country girl, your show is spot-on! Relatives, food, dumb people. You really are the funniest man. Thanks."

—Kimberly Bishop, Laurel, Indiana

"I am ninety-two years old, live alone, and have ailments that make for an uneasy existence. Life is not much fun, that is, until I watch your videos. You are a breath of fresh air and you make me feel good. You are a blessing."

—Jerry Bryant, Garland, Texas
(born and raised in West Virginia)

"I am home alone taking care of a husband with dementia and visual impairment. Your comedy videos are the only entertainment that bring him joy. I want to thank you for that. I applaud you for continuing to bring joy. Your talent is truly a blessing."

—A Fan, Georgia

"I call it commonsense comedy. Always makes me laugh and it's too bad you're not running for president!"

—James Johnson, Dubois, Wyoming

"I enjoy your stand-up comedy. Makes me laugh so loud and hard that sometimes I end up crying from laughter. Okay—I've peed."

—Marty, Mishawaka, Indiana

"I first listened to your comedy on a cassette tape that I think your sweet mama gave to my daddy because he was her hairdresser. He had no problem letting his thirteen-year-old daughter listen to clean comedy! I remember riding in the backseat of our family car going to a reunion and laughing so hard I could not breathe! Then when I got to the reunion, I looked around and wondered if you were a family member because your comedy is spot-on! Loved you and your hysterical mind for years!"

—Missy Mooneyham
Clark, Snellville, Georgia

"I found one of your posts on Facebook and thought, *Why not, I'll listen.* You not only made me laugh, you brought back memories as l could relate to your story. As time went on l kept listening, remembering and laughing. Thank you."

—A fan, Latrobe Valley, Victoria, Australia

"I have followed you for a long time and I will be driving 150 miles to see you this weekend in Myrtle Beach. Your comedy is second to no one and it's clean comedy. See you in Myrtle this weekend—and give a shout-out to the fat guy in the wheelchair!"

—Tracy Warden, Monroe, North Carolina

"Jerry Clower once said, 'I don't tell funny stories, I tell stories funny.' There is a difference and James Gregory is as great as Jerry Clower was in telling 'stories funny.' You are able to reach into my memories of childhood, of church potlucks, of fears of riding on an airplane (my grandfather said the problem with riding on an airplane is that you can't get out and check under the hood if there's a problem), of relative issues—and bring me into your world, as if you are peering through a window into my own world. You touch something deep inside me that says, *He knows, he knows. Preach on!*"

—David England, Campbellsville, Kentucky

"I've loved your stuff for a long time. While at my mission for months at a time in the Dominican Republic I listen to three or four sets every night. The laughter is a wonderful way to end the day."

—Bill Benson, Southern Ohio

"A personal friend of mine who lives in Delaware mentioned you to me. I listened to your show and laughed so hard I nearly had a stroke. I felt good about your routine because it was (if I may quote the woke crowd), 'an affirmation of the value of my kind of people'—which Hollywood and TV and Big Comedy usually scorn and disdain!"

—A fan, USA

"You make me yearn for the good ole days and rocking on my grandmother's porch. I first saw you in Anderson, South Carolina, and could not breathe during your relative-at-the-dinner-table bit. I smile when I think of you!! Thank you for the clean joy you spread!"

—Kelly Smith, Newberry, South Carolina

"I discovered your comedy shortly after our fifteen-year-old special needs son was called to Heaven because God needed special soldiers in his battles against the Devil. I was sinking into depression when a friend played one of your routines for me. I spent the next months playing a lot of your shows and they hit home. You taught me to smile again and I realized how great life is and that with comedy you can erase a lot of the negatives in your life. Thank you from the depths of my heart."

—Larry Moore, Ben Wheeler, Texas

"Mr. Gregory, I don't expect to be in your book, but I do not want to pass up the opportunity to tell you how much I love you. I am almost seventy-four years old and I don't know of any other comedian, ever, that can make me laugh the way that you do. No matter how bad I feel, if I put on one of your videos, you make me laugh until I cry. And for that I want to thank you. God bless you."

—A fan, Lexington, Kentucky

"My late father introduced me to your comedy with the fat-relative skit. He would tease me when I was in the kitchen with lines from it! He was suffering from cancer and this one joke made him happy. It's the only one we knew of at the time. We would swear you were talking about our family! This is exactly how they acted in the '70s. It's uncanny! Dad has since passed but I still get just as much joy out of that one skit in particular because it reminds me of him. I've never been so happy to be insulted in my life! I can still hear Dad yell, 'I'll take a stab at it!' And 'Don't throw that cornbread out!' You are a comedic genius and this joke will live on in my family."

—A fan, Owensboro, Kentucky

"My mom and dad are both gone, and all of my aunts and uncles that I grew up with. Your stories bring back all the ones I loved in those north

Georgia Hills, and in the north Alabama Hills. I knew those people. I knew those sayings."

—A fan, the American South

"My parents' family were from Alabama, and your humor and the lilt of your voice bring them back to life! I especially love your piece about the large aunt after a family get-together. I can just see my cousin and hear those same words coming from her mouth. You could have recorded her for your piece! We need so much more clean humor like yours."

—A fan, El Campo, Texas

"My favorite place to watch you is at the StarDome in Birmingham, Alabama. You seem at home here. I love the stories about the funerals and family dinners. I truly appreciate how much you make people laugh."

—Shari Calloway, Birmingham, Alabama

"I have lost two sons, a daughter, a grandson, and my husband of forty-four years. I never knew I could laugh again as hard as I do when I watch you. I think God let me find you. I have never been one to watch comedy but one day on YouTube there you were so I watched you—and I've been watching you every day, over and over, since I found you. I love the laughter you bring into my life and into my soul. The skits never get old, they just get funnier. The first thing I do in the morning drinking my coffee is turn on YouTube and find you and watch your skits all over again. I have fallen in love all over so thank you for that. Please keep doing what you're doing and keep bringing laughter to so many people that need it. I love you, and blessings to you and your family, and thank you."

—Lynda Gae Wilson, Nixa, Missouri

"Several years ago, you were checking in the Holiday Inn Express in Oxford, Alabama. My sister is the manager. She was checking you in, and when she caught your name, she was telling you how much I loved listening to you. She also told you how disappointed I was that I had to work that night and would miss your show you at the Alabama Show Palace that night. She called me at home and gave you the phone. I knew immediately who you were by the sound of your voice. You were ribbing me about missing your show. I said 'I sure do hate I'm going to miss it,' and you said, 'Well, call in!' I called my boss and told her you had called me on the phone. She said, 'Then you have to go! I'll work a double.' Not only are you funny, you are a very kind man with a soul to match."

—A fan, Alabama

"I never had a real family, but you, Mr. Gregory, made me a part of yours with your delightful way of bringing back memories of your own family. I love you dearly and if you ever get to come down my way I'll try and somehow fulfill my dream and go see you perform. Thanks for the memories, the love, and laughter that I only found with you."

—Alec, Mississippi

"Somewhere around 1990 your mama and my grandma met in a doctor's office waiting room and got to talking. After that they would talk and write often. Your mama sent grandma a VHS tape of your comedy performance. My grandparents, parents and I were all laughing 'til we had tears in our eyes. I can still hear their laughter and it is a memory that I will hold on to forever."

—A fan, Monticello, Georgia

"We saw you in '91 on your Tire Gauge tour in Savannah. We had been married about a year, and I had recently returned from Desert Storm, which had interrupted our formative married months. We both laughed so hard we could barely breathe, and moments from that show have been a significant part of the vernacular of our relationship ever since. Our boys knew you before they heard of you."

—Bill and Malinda Hoffmann
Smith, Elizabethton, Tennessee

"When my husband was diagnosed with multiple myeloma bone cancer in 2018, it was a devastating blow to our family. I would sit up late at night and watch him sleep in his lift chair 'cause the pain would not allow him to be comfortable in the bed. As I watched him sleep, I would cry and grieve cause I knew this diagnosis was not good. I found you, James, as I was thumbing through Facebook. I would listen to you and laugh on those nights as I cried and grieved over my husband. Your humor got me through some tough nights. I found out that you would be in Crossville at the Palace Theater so I purchased tickets and took my husband and four children with their spouses. We sat on the front row. What a treat to see you in person. Thanks for lifting up people and touching lives with your comedy in a way you know not."

—Mechelle Brown, Allardt, Tennessee

"With love from Australia…in this digital world, with thousands of miles between. You make my day bright. You have brought humor to me about the world in general and the people in it. No matter what sort of day I am having I can always rely on you to make me laugh and smile. Thank you so much for the fun."

—Ronald Bates, Warrnambool,
Victoria, Australia

"You are the apple in my pie. You are the cream in my coffee, the honey in my tea. You turn my crying into laughter. You make each day brighter. All the way from..."

—A fan, Cornwall, Ontario, Canada

"You are the funniest person I have ever heard and the fact that you accomplish this without being dirty, nasty, or blue is a true testament to the reason you have lasted so long. Thank you and may God bless you (and us) with many more years of your comedy."

—Jerry Brown, Indianapolis

"The first time I saw you, I laughed so hard my jaw hurt. I've enjoyed your comedy so many times since. I love how you find humor in the simple things and remind me not to take life so seriously."

—Eva Henderson, Morehead, Kentucky

"You, sir, are the greatest of American traditions south of the Mason-Dixie line, in the same glorious veins as the greats: Jerry Clower, Justin Wilson, Jeff Foxworthy, and Tim Wilson. They should put the five of y'all up on Stone Mountain in Georgia as a Mount Rushmore of comedians from the South."

—A fan, USA

"You sure made my day a lot of times when I was down and out. When I need a laugh after a bad day I look you up to raise my spirits."

—Joe Robinson, Canton, North Carolina

"You take me back to my childhood days growing up in Riverside and Bolton, Georgia. My grandmother and aunts and uncles always come to my mind when you tell your stories and I thank you for that!"

—Bob Huff, USA

"Your comedy has been a light in the darkness many times for me. I suffer from depression and anxiety and on my worst days I can watch you and it always helps to pull me back to reality. Thank you for that and for all you keep doing for everyone out there. You are a great man and comedian and I will forever be thankful for you."

—Mindy Hamm, Logan, Ohio

"Your comedy is not only funny but also thought provoking. You give something to think about—a mental mirror to ourselves. Every time I listen to you I not only laugh but I see just how things have and are changing, not always for the good. Thanks James for a great ride through this crazy thing called life."

—Nick Deonas, Fernandina Beach, Florida

"Your comedy is proof that you don't have to be nasty to be funny. I discovered you way too late in my life. Thanks to the power of the internet I have seen as much of your content as possible. The laughs and the jokes will live with me always. You are a treasure to comedy, sir."

—A fan, USA

"Your humor is so real. Everything you talk about has happened to people we all know—or to ourselves."

—Vickie Eads, Lebanon, Tennessee

"Your sense of humor has had me glued to your videos. I love the way you deliver the jokes! You truly have brought me so much laughter and joy. I think everyone can relate to many of your stories. One example: my husband died a year ago and it wasn't a full week I had three or four men ask me what I was going to do with his pickup truck. In the midst of my grief, I chuckled each time. True story. Thanks for the memories!"

—Ann Cox, Corpus Christi, Texas

"You're the funniest man in the whole world, not only in 'Murica. I love comedy, and laughter takes my stress away. And I am thankful to encounter you here. Hugs and lots of love from…"

—A fan, Narita, Japan

ACKNOWLEDGMENTS

R on DiNunzio and Dave Montesanto (without whom I would not be in the comedy business), Chris DiPetta, Tony Kemp, Aubrey Pippen, Bruce Ayers (one of a kind), Jay Leno, Steven Wright, Russ Fisher, Ralph Emery (the Johnny Carson of The Nashville Network), Bill Cody (WSM radio in Nashville), Bobby Cudd (Monterrey Artists), Judi Brown Marmel, Susan Cox (my right arm), Jeff Foxworthy, Larry Black (Gabriel Communications), Steve Pritchard, Jeff Gilstrap, Dr. Paul Howard (Birmingham, AL), Melissa Allen (my attorney), Ray Stevens (when he was inducted into the Country Music Hall of Fame, it was my honor to participate in the ceremony), Brett Butler, Dolly Parton, Lenny Sisselman (my manager and solid as a rock), Bernie Cook (he's been my CPA and tax adviser for almost forty years), Mike Long (who worked with me to write this story of my life), Rhubarb Jones, Jimmy Hammett, Dennis Hopper (he said to me "Your mind is as sharp as mine is demented"), Dr. Heather Silver (my physician), Dr. Adam Mitchell (my cardiologist), Bill Anderson (legendary singer and songwriter—I love him, and my sister was obsessed with him), Mark Thompson (my first and still the easiest promoter to work with), Les McCurdy and Ken Sons (the founders and original owners of The Comedy Catch in Chattanooga, TN), Craig Wilson (the guy who is responsible for the trips I made to Canada to perform, and as he said, "Show Canadians what funny is all about"), Dan Miller (legendary news anchor and broadcaster in Nashville, TN at WSMV TV), Randy Travis, John Boy & Billy and entire production team—Marci, Jackie, and Randy (syndicated radio, Charlotte, NC), Rick & Bubba (syndicated radio, Birmingham, AL), Bob & Tom (syndicated radio, Indianapolis, IN), Matt McCoy and Mike Reeves (Excelsior Mill comedy workshop), Al Searcy and Brian Quinn (my financial planners), Ritch Shydner (he has a master's degree in stand-up comedy), Robert (Robo) Walker, Randy Williams, Brian Dorfman (the owner of Zanies in Nashville, TN), Bruce Plante (a political cartoonist who created the James Gregory caricature), Bob Johnson (a long-running news anchor and broadcaster in Chattanooga, TN), first responders/paramedics (they've been my chauffeurs several different times in Georgia, Alabama, and North Carolina), Fred de Cordova (producer of *The Tonight Show With Johnny Carson*), J. Anthony Brown (he can do it all and do it well—stand-up, radio, television and movies), Keith Bilbrey, Gerald Kubach and Mike Kutash (the founders of the Funny Bone empire), Tommy Williams (owner of the original Charlie Goodnights comedy club in Raleigh, NC), Steve Mingolla, Vinnie Coppola and Dan Mengini (my own Three Musketeers—three funny, professional Italians), Austin Myers (there's not enough words to describe who and what he is), Brad Greenberg (founder of the Comedy Zone comedy club chain—we've been friends since 1984. It bothers me that he doesn't get the respect and gratitude he's entitled to), and Dean Gaines (a rare human being and a professional, successful entertainer!).

ADDITIONAL ACKNOWLEDGMENTS

Every day of my life, I remind myself that the house I live in and the cars I drive were paid for by the fans of stand-up comedy. The shoes I wear and the clothes I have on were paid for by the fans of stand-up comedy. The groceries in my cupboard and the porterhouse steaks in my freezer were paid for by the fans of stand-up comedy.